Legal Interpreting and Questioning Techniques Explained

Language and law are closely linked, and language is fundamental to the application of the law. Legal, criminalistic, translational and psychological aspects of communication come together in interpreted questioning (hearings, interrogations, interviews) and must be taken into account, especially since the way in which the questioning outcomes are evaluated can have far-reaching legal consequences. Building on empirical studies and practice, this accessible text provides a transdisciplinary examination of questioning methods and strategies. The institutional framework conditions of a questioning situation are examined in the context of transdisciplinary cooperation.

This book also addresses the increasing use of technology and hybrid forms of translation and interpreting in the legal system, and shows different ways in which interpreters co-construct information. Chapters include summaries of key concepts and definitions, examples from existing literature combined with practical experience and the results of surveys conducted by the authors, as well as further reading and non-language-specific study activities. Activities include role plays on thematic scenarios involving different actors in criminal proceedings and discussion groups to enable reflection on ethical issues and discursive challenges.

This is a vital text for both advanced students and professionals in interpreting studies and criminology.

Mira Kadrić is professor for Interpreting Studies and Didactics of Translation at the University of Vienna, Austria. Her research focuses especially on empirical work on interpreting, drawing on her experience as an interpreter for the courts, public services and political institutions.

Monika Stempkowski is a postdoctoral researcher at the University of Vienna, Austria. Her research focuses on questions of legal psychology, mentally ill perpetrators, illicit drugs and prison studies. She is registered as a clinical and health psychologist and as a certified mediator.

Ivana Havelka is a postdoctoral researcher at the University of Vienna, Austria. Her research interests include dialogue interpreting and technology-mediated interpreting, with a focus on legal contexts. She has over a decade of experience as a court interpreter in Austria.

Translation Practices Explained
Series Editor: Kelly Washbourne

Translation Practices Explained is a series of coursebooks designed to help self-learners and students on translation and interpreting courses. Each volume focuses on a specific aspect of professional translation and interpreting practice, usually corresponding to courses available in translator- and interpreter-training institutions. The authors are practicing translators, interpreters, and/or translator or interpreter trainers. Although specialists, they explain their professional insights in a manner accessible to the wider learning public.

Each volume includes activities and exercises designed to help learners consolidate their knowledge, while updated reading lists and website addresses will also help individual learners gain further insight into the realities of professional practice.

Most recent titles in the series:

Medical Translation Step by Step
Learning by Drafting
Vicent Montalt, Maria González-Davies

Translation-Driven Corpora
Corpus Resources for Descriptive and Applied Translation Studies
Federico Zanettin

Indirect Translation Explained
Hanna Pięta, Rita Bueno Maia and Ester Torres-Simón

Translation, Adaptation and Digital Media
John Milton and Silvia Cobelo

Legal Interpreting and Questioning Techniques Explained
Mira Kadrić, Monika Stempkowski and Ivana Havelka

For more information on any of these and other titles, or to order, please go to www.routledge.com/Translation-Practices-Explained/book-series/TPE

Additional resources for Translation and Interpreting Studies are available on the Routledge Translation Studies Portal: http://routledgetranslationstudiesportal.com

Legal Interpreting and Questioning Techniques Explained

Mira Kadrić, Monika Stempkowski and Ivana Havelka

English edited by Sylvi Rennert

Routledge
Taylor & Francis Group
LONDON AND NEW YORK

Designed cover image: Mira Kadrić

First published 2024
by Routledge
4 Park Square, Milton Park, Abingdon, Oxon OX14 4RN

and by Routledge
605 Third Avenue, New York, NY 10158

Routledge is an imprint of the Taylor & Francis Group, an informa business

British Library Cataloguing-in-Publication Data
A catalogue record for this book is available from the British Library

ISBN: 978-1-032-29443-8 (hbk)
ISBN: 978-1-032-29441-4 (pbk)
ISBN: 978-1-003-30158-5 (ebk)

DOI: 10.4324/9781003301585

Typeset in Times New Roman
by Apex CoVantage, LLC

Access the Support Material: http://routledgetranslationstudiesportal.com

Contents

Figures

Acknowledgements

We would like to take this opportunity to express our gratitude to everyone who contributed to the creation of this textbook.

First and foremost, our thanks go to Sylvi Rennert for her translation and editing work on this book. Her support not only improved the quality of the text but also helped make complex topics understandable and accessible. As a member of the Vienna research group TransLaw, Sylvi also shared her scientific expertise and contributed valuable ideas and suggestions in our discussions during the writing process – thank you!

Special thanks are extended to Alexandra Braunesberger und Simone Uran for their assistance with the illustrations in this book.

Lastly, we would like to thank everyone at Routledge for their support during the development of this volume.

Abbreviations

CBCA	Criteria-Based Content Analysis
CFR	European Charter of Fundamental Rights
ECHR	European Convention for the Protection of Human Rights and Fundamental Freedoms
ECtHR	European Court of Human Rights
EU	European Union
EUROPOL	European Union Agency for Law Enforcement Cooperation
ICESCR	International Covenant on Economic, Social and Cultural Rights
ICCPR	International Covenant on Civil and Political Rights
ICT	Information and Communication Technology
ICTR	International Criminal Tribunal for Rwanda
ICTY	The International Criminal Tribunal for the former Yugoslavia
INTERPOL	International Criminal Police Organization
UNHCR	UN High Commissioner for Refugees

Introduction

Language and law are closely linked, and language is fundamental to the application of the law. Legal, criminalistic, translatorial and psychological aspects of communication come together in interpreted *questioning* (hearings, interviews, interrogations) and all need to be considered, especially since the way in which the *questioning* outcomes are evaluated can have far-reaching legal consequences. Building on empirical studies and practice, this publication provides a transdisciplinary examination of *questioning* methods and strategies. The institutional framework conditions of a *questioning* situation are examined in the context of transdisciplinary cooperation. This book also addresses the increasing use of technology and hybrid forms of translation and interpreting in the legal system, and shows different ways in which interpreters co-construct information.

As the demand for interpreting in public institutions increases, so does awareness of it, which must inevitably lead to increased transdisciplinary academic interest. Discourse today centres on areas such as co-education, common minimum standards, working conditions for on-site and remote interpreting, training programmes and ethical issues, suggesting that court and public interpreting is highly relevant both in practice and in research. Transdisciplinary collaboration is becoming increasingly important. The cooperation of interpreters and legal experts is especially relevant when it comes to interviews and *questioning* as an essential act of communication in legal proceedings, and is therefore our focus. Successful cooperation or the lack thereof affects the *questioning* situation. *Questioning* as a form of institutional communication is complex and places a number of professional and psychological demands on those involved in the communicative situation. Finally, the increasingly rapid developments in information and communication technology – not least as a consequence of the global pandemic – are also changing private and institutional communication. The addition of an interpreter changes the dynamics of a *questioning* situation.

The use of communication technology (ICT) for interpreting originates in countries with large distances, such as Australia, Brazil or the US. Technology makes it possible to meet the demands of high interpreting needs and rare language combinations.

The book's focus is on interpreting strategies and *questioning* techniques. *Questioning* defendants, victims and witnesses constitutes one of the core elements of

DOI: 10.4324/9781003301585-1

any criminal proceedings. While for the police, the court and the prosecution, the focus lies on establishing the truth in order to reach a verdict, the main goal of the accused is to defend themselves. Therefore, different interests prevail in this situation and require professionalism and a comprehensive education of interpreters providing their services within this setting as well as of police officers and judges. The *questioning* situations differ between countries, and in particular between adversarial and the *inquisitorial systems*. These fundamental differences between *case law* and *civil law* and their relevance for *questioning* (and interpreting) are discussed as well.

In order to avoid the issue of terminological differences in different languages and legal systems, we use the term *questioning*; for all forms of communication where one person answers the questions of one or more persons who have been authorised to do so by a public authority (including hearings, interviews, examinations, interrogations, cross-examinations, depositions etc.). The umbrella term *questioning* and the terms it corresponds to in specific countries or legal systems are addressed in the study activities.

We strive to make statements about translation generally applicable, regardless of whether they pertain to spoken or sign languages and regardless of legal systems, and predominantly employ the terminology from ISO 20228:2019 on Interpreting services – Legal interpreting.

The study activities are based on transdisciplinary work and mutual learning. They use individual learning and learning in *tandem*, or pairs, but also encompass the methods of role-play and simulations. All forms of interaction are suited for practising work with content, texts, situations, persons, intentions and emotions.

To avoid cluttering the text with sources, references will be provided at the end of each respective chapter. Where necessary, sources will be cited directly within the text.

Sources

International Organization for Standardization. (no date). 'Interpreting services: Legal interpreting: Requirements Services d'interprétation: Interprétation juridique et judiciaire — Exigences', ISO 20228 https://www.iso.org/standard/67327.html (accessed 27 September 2023).

1 Questioning and interpreting as special forms of communication

Chapter summary

Both *questioning* and *interpreting* are special forms of communication. This chapter describes the areas of application, actors and examples of communicative situations with and without the use of technology that involve (interpreted) *questioning*. We describe settings such as police interviews and *questioning* in court, and discuss the typical participants and particular characteristics of these settings. We explain the roles and role expectations of all actors and the interpreting techniques that can be used in each setting. Study activities in this chapter include analysis and discussions of the country-specific settings and forms of legal communication.

1.1 Questioning as a key component of legal communication

Being heard in a legal matter and having the opportunity to communicate are the basic requirements for a fair trial. Therefore, communication is an inextricable part of exercising one's rights and meeting one's obligations in legal proceedings. Access to justice through successful communication is the result of the joint efforts of all persons involved in the communication. Therefore, interpreting not only serves to ensure successful communication between at least two communicators, but also makes participation in the legal process possible in the first place. The legal and translation professions share the challenge of facilitating well-functioning and equitable communication in fair proceedings.

With their work, interpreters support the communication of legal professionals. In order for legal professionals and interpreters to cooperate successfully, it is crucial that they understand each other's areas of responsibility and objectives. The objectives may vary depending on the setting. Previous studies of *questioning* situations show that joint preparation, cooperation and understanding the requirements a *questioning* situation poses for the interpreting process improve the interpreting output and thus the *questioning* outcomes.

DOI: 10.4324/9781003301585-2

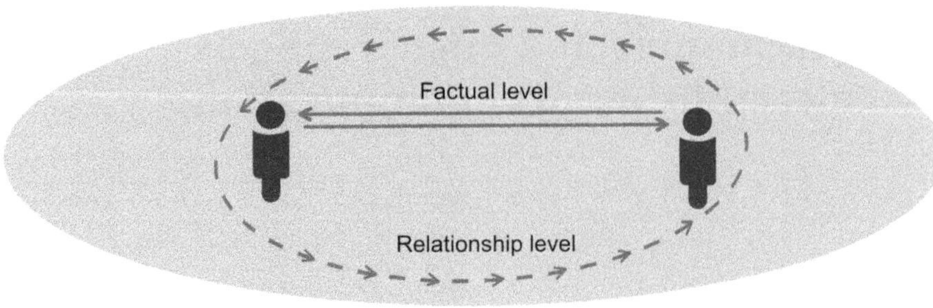

Figure 1.1 One-to-one communication

Language itself is a holistic tapestry woven from flexible materials, taking on diverse shapes across various linguistic and cultural contexts. In linguistic usage, we observe the embodiment of entrenched values, life circumstances, the specific environment or the (specialised) context produced by the individuals and their actions. All languages have in common a use of various communicative symbols, here represented as three inseparable components of a single tool: the linguistic realm, encompassing the exchange of verbal elements like words, sentences or signs, including intonation, tempo and rhythm; and the non-verbal dimension, which extends to cues such as posture, gaze and body language, as well as extralinguistic elements, which include the spatial context, role distribution and other external attributes. This includes, for example, the architecture and design of spaces in official buildings or visible attributes of position, such as a robe or wig.

Language is thus used holistically and synchronously, incorporating all communicative elements consciously or unconsciously, and is transmitted as a single communicative act. Ideally, the interlocutor understands these elements the way the sender intended them. This assumption holds true for individuals who communicate in the same language and share comparable background knowledge.

Questioning is a key component of legal communication in any criminal investigation and criminal proceedings, not only from a legal but also from a translatorial perspective. Typical examples of *questioning* include police interviews, interrogations by the public prosecutor's office and hearings in court.

However, many elements and principles of the *questioning* settings described in this book can be applied to similar settings in other areas of law, such as civil or family law, or other settings that have a similar *questioning* setup, such as in a court of arbitration, before competition or anti-trust authorities, but also in interviews at youth welfare offices or in asylum proceedings.

It makes no difference whether the institutions involved are national (e.g. police, court), supranational (e.g. EU) or intergovernmental (e.g. Interpol).

Although *questioning* is an unusual situation for most individuals, it is, at its core, something people are confronted with on a daily basis in a wide range of settings and constellations: *questioning* is always a communication process. Therefore, the dynamics and rules of *questioning* situations are often the same that apply to communicative settings in general and have been studied in depth by social psychologists.

Nevertheless, there are some ways in which *questioning* situations differ fundamentally from other communication processes. This is due to the roles of the people involved. The person asking the questions has the professional role of *questioner*, and therefore has options and instruments at her disposal that are not available to the *questionee*. Consider, for example, that in some legal systems, witnesses in criminal proceedings are obliged to testify, and refusal to do so may result in penalties. The *questioner* is also, however, subject to strict legal rules that limit his possibilities and guide his actions. Unlike communication processes in personal or professional environments, *questioning* situations are subject to a host of norms and laws. The *questionee* generally cannot decide for herself whether she wants to participate or not. This makes a *questioning* situation a form of coercive communication, which naturally impacts the social dynamics of the situation and should be kept in mind by the *questioner* (and the interpreter). What is the goal of *questioning*? When can you say *questioning* has been successful? The aim of *questioning* is to obtain information in order to establish the truth of the matter. Obtaining information to establish the truth is the objective of *questioning* not only in criminal and administrative proceedings, but also in civil proceedings. Although the parties in civil proceedings usually have more options than in criminal proceedings, *questioning* by the court must still always seek to establish what really happened.

We distinguish between dyadic and triadic communication. Dyadic communication refers to communication between two parties in a shared language.

Because of the different roles, objectives and levels of knowledge of the communicators, dyadic communication in legal settings does not work in a linear manner. Generally speaking, however, the main dimensions of any communicative situation can be located at two levels, regardless of the communicators' roles: the factual level and the relationship level. Information is exchanged at the factual level, but the factual and the relationship levels are closely interwoven, thus influencing how *translatorial rapport* is established.

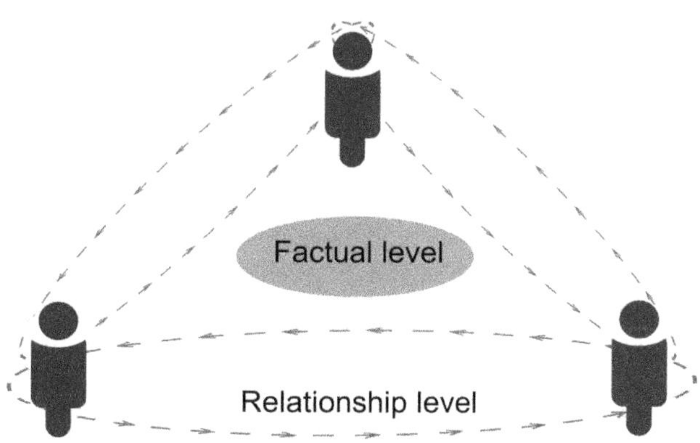

Figure 1.2 One-to-two communication

Language itself is a holistic compound of different levels of information, which are determined by the environment, the context, and the parties involved and their behaviour. Language as a phenomenon, therefore, occurs not only at the linguistic level, with verbal elements such as words, sentences and signs, but also at the para-verbal level, with the information transmitted by intonation, rhythm or the tempo of speech, as well as at the non-verbal level, with cues such as posture, gaze and body, and the extra-linguistic level, which can convey information through body language, spatial behaviour or clothes.

Information is therefore conveyed and also received simultaneously on multiple channels. If an interpreter is needed, this changes the way the communication is organised: the dyad becomes a triad. In a triad, a third person becomes part of the communication without being a primary communicator. The resulting **triadic communication** is a constellation that is unnatural from the perspective of the primary communicators and requires adaptations in their communication behaviour.

All communication is multimodal, and the interlocutor processes the verbal, prosodic and non-verbal elements together with extra-linguistic information to understand the meaning of an utterance. In a triad with an interpreter, communication is no longer synchronous, as the end user receives the meaning of the words with a delay, uncoupled from the prosodic, non-verbal and extra-linguistic cues. This changes the dynamics of communication.

In *questioning* situations, the separate transmission of verbal and non-verbal information can be a hindrance. In addition, the fact that the primary communicators no longer communicate directly and their communication needs to be facilitated by the interpreter can make it harder to build trust and thus to establish rapport, i.e. to create trust-based and ultimately successful communication. Especially since *questioning* situations contain a coercive element, establishing rapport between *questioner* and *questionee* is of great importance in order to increase the chances of obtaining useful information. In interpreted *questioning* situations, the *questioner* therefore has to apply additional effort to build a working relationship with the *questionee*. Interpreting studies distinguishes between different forms of phatic communication, which are used to start, prolong, interrupt or end the communicative situation; the role of phatic communication in building *translatorial rapport* in interpreted settings will be addressed later in this book.

1.2 Interpreting in service of people and institutions

Interpreting is done in the service of human beings. In the institutional context, interpreting is generally an indispensable service for those involved. The social or professional status of the communicators is irrelevant to the interpreter in the provision of their service. The status of someone as representing an institution or being a party to legal proceedings is only relevant to the interpreter where it directly affects their communicative needs. From the perspective of the interpreter, people who speak different languages meet, exchange information and need to be able to communicate without problems. Communicating is important not only for the individuals involved but also for the functioning of the institution in question. In other words, interpreting serves people and institutions.

Interpreting is conveying information from a signed or spoken source language into a signed or spoken target language. The source language content can be spoken, signed or written.

In interpreting, we distinguish between the modes of consecutive and simultaneous interpreting. Simultaneous interpreting happens while the speaker is uttering the source information, while consecutive interpreting is done once the speaker has finished.

Regardless of the interpreting mode, the speech segments to be interpreted can vary in length, ranging from a single word or sentence to longer, thematically coherent statements from one speaker. In administrative contexts or *questioning* situations, typical examples of short segments are question/answer sequences with consecutive interpreting after each speaker, while longer segments might include free narration of their experience presented without interruptions by the *questionee*, which are interpreted consecutively in what is called long consecutive, using notes.

The communicative units adhere to the principles of orality: utterances may be incomplete or contain linguistic errors, interruptions or leaps in thought may occur, and language may be accompanied or even replaced by non-verbal and paraverbal elements, etc.

There are also hybrid forms, such as *sight interpreting*, where a written text is interpreted into a different language as a spoken or signed text, or the transfer of spoken or signed information into a written form, either simultaneously, such as in speech-to-text interpreting or live subtitling, or with a delay, such as in communication surveillance.

In this book, we focus on consecutive interpreting in predominantly dialogic communicative settings, as used in the core areas discussed here, i.e. criminal investigations, criminal proceedings, and, in particular, in police and court interpreting. In consecutive interpreting, the interpreter hears or sees the information in the source language, processes it and then interprets it after the speaker has finished, i.e. consecutively. Interpreters store the source information at two levels: at the cognitive level in their short-term memory and in material form as notes on a digital or analogue notepad.

Consecutive interpreting is primarily used in communicative situations with a usually small number of participants. The situations discussed here have a clear structure of question and response. They might take place in an office where someone is interviewed about a situation, at a police station to find out how a crime unfolded, at the public prosecutor's office where a suspect is questioned, or at court to establish the truth of the matter by *questioning* witnesses, defendants or expert witnesses.

In these situations, people usually word their utterances freely, even if they have been prepared in advance. They are predominantly dialogic, i.e. people communicate directly; initiating utterances are followed by reactive utterances. Due to their dynamic nature, dialogues can take an unexpected turn at any time, and they may contain ambiguities or contradictions.

Communicators use body language to support, add to or replace verbal utterances. In dialogic settings, body language is usually directed at the interlocutor and may serve to include them or to show attention. The person who is currently not speaking will often indicate attention through feedback cues such as body language (e.g. nodding). This strengthens the relationship between the parties to the communication, and is in contrast to monologic texts, such as an opening statement or a pronouncement of a judgment, where the speaker's body language reinforces the message and is often used unintentionally, and feedback cues are not generally expected.

It also makes a difference whether one person is asking the questions or there are several *questioner*s. Compare, for example, a situation at a police station where a single police officer is *questioning* the suspect, with a courtroom, where the presiding judge questions the defendant, but the members of the jury, the prosecution, defenders and legal representatives of victims also have the right to ask questions. In such a situation, the relationship level fades into the background and the factual level between the *questionee* and the various *questioners* is foregrounded.

Consecutive interpreting in legal settings can also include monologic texts, i.e. where one speaker gives a complete statement or speech, which are typically longer than parts of a dialogue. Reading the charges to the defendant or pronouncing the judgment is generally monologic speech, with unidirectional communication. Monologic communication has the advantage for the interpreter that there are generally no changes in topic and the content is to some extent predictable. *Legal interpreting* settings can present a combination of monologic and dialogic communication, e.g. when the reading of the charges is followed by *questioning*.

Although interpreting as social interaction takes place at the linguistic level, the interpreting process extends beyond this level and requires consideration of the holistic interaction of verbal, non-verbal and extra-linguistic cues. These may include context cues, which can depend on the legal culture or culture-specific concepts. They contribute significantly to the meaning of what is said. The task of the interpreter, therefore, is to consider not only language barriers, but also cultural barriers. Culture can become evident in the form of a multimodal expression, where verbal

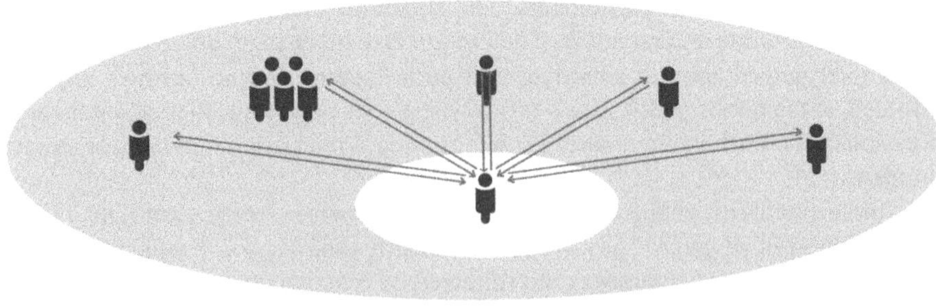

Figure 1.3 Many-to-one communication

and non-verbal communication elements combine to form meaning. Interpreting, therefore, takes place not only at the linguistic level – it is a holistic communicative approach.

In this holistic approach, the linguistic material is considered part of a whole. This means that interpreting always also considers the function that the interpretation is intended to fulfil for the end users. This shows that interpreting includes culture-specific and situation-, time-, purpose- and context-dependent aspects in addition to the relevant verbal elements. After all, interpreting for courts and public authorities has real impacts on the lives of people, as they not only participate passively in the proceedings but shape them actively, exercising their legal rights and duties. Language is not only communication; it is an action (Wadensjö, 1998).

Legal interpreting covers a range of settings related to law and legal matters. We can distinguish by type of setting (judicial or extrajudicial) and by client (public entity or private person/entity).

Judicial interpreting takes place at courts, tribunals and public prosecutors at national, international, supranational or intergovernmental levels, and can be seen as part of court and public service interpreting. It can be subdivided by area of jurisdiction, i.e. criminal, civil or administrative courts, and encompasses all situations connected to court proceedings, from *questioning* by the police, the public prosecutor or the judge to appearances in court, arraignment on the indictment, where the accused is formally informed of the charges against them, bail hearings, the trial itself and the sentencing. At the international and supranational levels, interpreting is needed by courts such as the International Criminal Court, the European Court of Justice, the African Court on Human and Peoples' Rights, the Inter-American Court of Human Rights or the European Court of Human Rights.

Extrajudicial settings are all settings outside of court or public prosecutors' offices. This includes interpreting for public authorities such as the police (when no court case is involved, e.g. traffic violations), in asylum hearings and in administrative matters such as applications for licences and permits or recognition

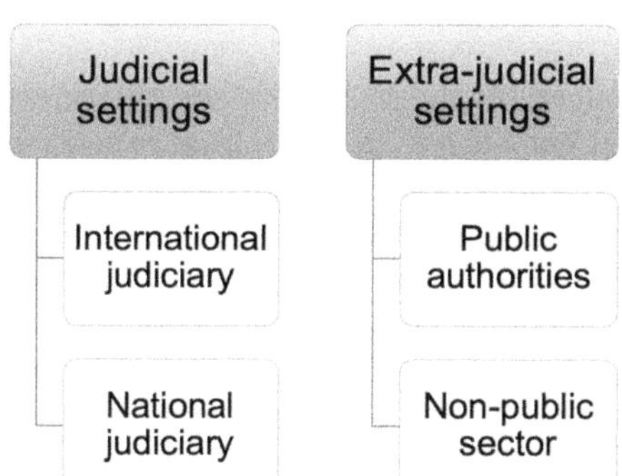

Figure 1.4 Questioning in legal settings

of degrees acquired abroad, but also interpreting in the non-public sector, such as contract negotiations, legal consultations with lawyers or notaries, mediation procedures and other legal extrajudicial situations with private clients. While interpreting for clients in the non-public sector is not always regulated by law in scope nor in fee, interpreting for public authorities and courts is generally governed by legal regulations for the use of interpreters, as discussed above, as well as rules at the legal or institutional level that regulate all matters relating to interpreting, often including the fee. In some settings, participation is strictly regulated and legal activity is reserved for notaries, lawyers etc., while other sectors allow unreserved legal activity. This concerns questions such as providing legal counsel or defending someone in court, and may therefore also be relevant to the activities interpreters are allowed to perform.

Although interpreting and translation are different activities, legal interpreters often also provide translations of documents or contracts, especially where the documents refer to a case they are interpreting for. The *sight interpreting* of written texts, where the interpreter provides an oral rendition of a document in another language, however, is considered part of interpreting, and is common practice. This may include documents such as indictments, arrest warrants or court settlements. The translation or interpreting of police telephone surveillance can also be considered part of court interpreting.

1.3 Actors and the power of discourse

Interpreters enable communication between two or more parties who would otherwise not be able to communicate, at least not to the extent desired. While the interpreter seeks to provide comprehension and communication for all parties involved, the parties themselves may have different, overlapping or even identical interests. In a criminal case, for example, a defendant consulting with their defence counsel and working on a strategy to achieve acquittal have a shared interest, but the defendant and the prosecutor have conflicting interests: while the prosecutor is bringing the charges and seeking a sentence, the defendant and their counsel are generally seeking acquittal or a mild sentence. The judge is interested in the fair conduct of the proceedings and, depending on the legal system, *questioning* the parties or trying to determine the truth.

In addition to the potentially diverging interests, the participants may also have different levels of legal knowledge: in court, legal experts such as lawyers, prosecutors or judges communicate with persons who have no legal training, such as witnesses, defendants or expert witnesses, or who have some knowledge of legal proceedings but are not experts, such as members of the police. Differences in interests and legal knowledge can also occur in all other areas of *legal interpreting*, e.g. in contract negotiations between two companies, where one is familiar with the local laws, or when filing for a building permit at the competent office. Here, the administrative staff may not have legal training, but they are familiar with the area of law they work in. Situations where no trained legal experts are present at all are also possible, but not the subject of this book.

The end users, i.e. court officials, governmental or non-governmental entities, or private individuals, are responsible for the communication and its outcome, but they rely on the interpreter's service as an expert who makes the legal and the factual understandable in their languages. They cannot judge the interpreter's performance, but nevertheless have to place trust in them to enable communication. The interpreting situation is therefore an interaction between at least three persons–two primary communicators and the interpreter–who are all equally important to the communication process and its results but may have divergent interests and knowledge.

The institution of *questioning*, its participant configurations and communication dynamics represent a special type of (interpreted) communication. In most cases, it involves communicators who do not have a common objective nor the same level of knowledge. Such configurations provide an ideal space for attempts at manipulation, exerting influence and exercising social and institutional power.

Institutional communication involves undeniable institutional power that is exercised and reproduced in and through the interpretation. This is the case, in particular, in interpreting for courts and authorities (e.g. police, public prosecutors, courts). The (legal) experts are well-versed in institutional discourse and institutional communication, while the other parties are usually not familiar with the pragmatic use of language in institutional settings. The use of legal language in discourse gives control to the institution.

The distribution of power in the discourse is one-sided; the institutional structure of communication, especially in *questioning* situations, dictates turn taking. The *questioner* also controls the content and steers the conversation according to the task she has been given by the institution and the communicative goal resulting from this. The *questioner* is endowed with institutional authority, which witnesses and parties to the proceedings lack. The *questioner* typically steers the conversation and the exchange of information. Interruptions are generally purposeful, e.g. to control the course of *questioning*.

The distribution of power and hierarchies permeates all dimensions of communication. They are not necessarily expressed verbally in direct communication but may be visible in extralinguistic factors. They are effective by virtue of the awareness of their existence and effect: It is sufficient to know that someone has the power to make decisions that would affect us positively or negatively to increase the chances of us complying–in addition to fundamental institutional power that can enforce coercive communication, e.g. the obligation to testify.

1.4 Requirements and expectations

The objective of interpreting is to facilitate communication between the primary interlocutors as if there were no language barrier.

In order to enable communication, interpreters must know and consider the plans, scope of action, objectives and interests of all primary communicators, taking into account linguistic, professional and cultural aspects as essential elements, as they are directly linked to communication.

In addition to linguistic, professional and, in some cases, cultural barriers that need to be bridged, there are a number of situational factors that influence (interpreted) communication, such as time, purpose, atmosphere, type of *questioning*, the emotional state of the participants and more.

The art of interpreting is to convey the information in the best way possible for very different end users (representatives of public authorities and private individuals) and to make the 'source material' available to the primary communicators in such a way that the parties can speak for themselves and the authorities receive all the information that has been presented to make their decisions. In criminal proceedings, for example, it is not sufficient for the defendant to be just physically present in the courtroom. In order for him to be meaningfully present ('linguistic presence'), everything that is said in the proceedings must be communicated to him in a language and form that he can understand. The relevant legal provisions are explained in the next chapter.

Interpreters act *multipartially* and in keeping with the communicative intentions of all primary communicators.

The concept of *multipartiality* was originally developed for the field of mediation. The fundamental requirements for *multipartiality* in interpreting are the independence and unbiased approach of the interpreter, allowing them to be impartial and multipartial at once.

In a legal context, a distinction can be made between partiality, *multipartiality* and impartiality. A lawyer is generally partial, while the role of the judge is to be impartial. To be impartial, they naturally also need to be independent and unbiased. The judge must stand above the disputing parties, expert witnesses, interpreters and other participants in the proceedings and uphold the rights. of all parties in a balanced manner.

The concept of *multipartiality* has several aspects that are of relevance for interpreters, whose task is to mediate at both the linguistic and cultural levels between parties with different interests. The principle of *multipartiality* relieves interpreters of the usually impossible task of trying to meet the often conflicting goals of the parties involved. Equidistance allows interpreters to distance themselves from the parties in a way that serves the interests of all communicators and protects the interpreter themselves from being open to attacks because of their position at the centre of communication. In doing so, interpreters participate in an objective way without becoming involved in the contents of the case. The unbiased attitude of the interpreter and their equal distance (but also equal proximity) to all communicators creates an attitude of *multipartiality*.

End users often expect the interpreter to assume their point of view and to take their side or speak for them. Indeed, interpreters do sometimes have to intervene to add explanations, ask questions when they have not understood something or point out misunderstandings; however, these interventions serve the communication and not the personal interests of any parties.

After all, an utterance is never an isolated communicative unit, but a link in a semantic chain, and it can therefore only be considered and understood in light of the situational and professional context. The success of interpreted *questioning* situations inevitably depends on understanding the overall context and the possibilities and limits of interpreting.

Therefore, interpreting cannot be seen as a purely linguistic transfer – the linguistic material is understood as part of the whole. That means that interpreting is always done with regard to the function that the interpretation is supposed to fulfil for the particular purpose, norm and end users.

1.5 The impact of technology on communication

Technologies both facilitate and change communication. The development of information and communication technology is increasingly changing communication in the legal field. Communication adapts to the possibilities and limitations of the technology used. Due to the limitations to the communicative situation, technology-assisted communication is different than communication without technology, in particular in terms of what can be perceived and ways of interacting. As a result, distance interpreting differs from on-site interpreting.

Two basic modes of distance interpreting are used in the legal context: remote interpreting, where the interpreter is remote and primary communicators are all in one place, and teleconference interpreting, where the primary communicators are in different locations and connected via audio and/or video, with the interpreter at one of these locations or at a separate location. The latter, the so-called multipoint interpreting setup where everyone is in a separate location, was especially common during the pandemic to avoid the risk of infection.

The use of technology can easily shift power or create new forms of asymmetrical power, generally in favour of the institution, while the other party, who is connected remotely, loses power. Remote technology-assisted interpreting also limits the action space of the interpreter, leading to a loss of control and power over the source information. The limitations remote interpreting places on the perception of information and other people involved in the proceedings means that the interpreter is faced with a lack of information that can impact the interpreting output and may have negative consequences for the end user (usually the party who does not speak the *language of service*). For interpreters themselves, this can lead to social and institutional 'isolation'.

The use of information and communications technology (ICT) is governed by legal norms such as EU Directive 2010/64 on the right to interpretation and translation in criminal proceedings, which explicitly says that videoconferencing, telephone or the internet may be used 'unless the physical presence of the interpreter is required in order to safeguard the fairness of the proceedings ICT is increasingly used worldwide for internal and external communication of courts and authorities, accelerated by the measures to prevent the spread of Covid-19. For interpreters who work in the field of remote interpreting, it quickly becomes evident that there are significant differences compared to on-site interpreting. Challenge lies in the perception (e.g. limited field of vision) and interaction with the end users (harder to use non-verbal cues) and leads to a loss of empathic connection.

Study activities

- *Settings*
  - List which judicial and extra-judicial settings you know in your country that regularly use interpreting.
  - Discuss in small groups your list of judicial and extra-judicial settings in your country.
  - Following this, give an example of a judicial or extra-judicial setting that you have observed or participated in.
  - Outline the actors in the respective setting and analyse the requirements and expectations of the setting.
- *Communication analysis in pairs*

  Preparation: In *tandems* (pairs), choose a specific communication scenario that involves *questioning*, such as a video clip or a scene from a film.

Pay close attention to the interplay between verbal, non-verbal and extra-linguistic elements. Analyse these elements as belonging to either the factual level or the relationship level of communication:

Factual level: Identify and outline the elements of communication that pertain to the factual content of the dialogue. This includes what is explicitly stated or asked.

Relationship level: Examine the elements that contribute to the relational dynamics between the communicators. This could include tone, body language and other non-verbal cues.

By completing this task, you will gain a nuanced understanding of how different elements contribute to the overall communication process, especially in contexts that involve *questioning*.

Sources and further reading

Braun, S. and Taylor, J.L. (eds.) (2012) *Videoconference and Remote Interpreting in Criminal Proceedings*. Cambridge: Intersentia.

French, J.R.P. Jr. and Raven, B.H. (1959) 'The Bases of Social Power' in Cartwright, D. (ed.) *Studies in Social Power*. Ann Arbor, MI: Institute for Social Research, pp. 150–67.

Havelka, I., Iacono, K., Pöllabauer, S. and Stachl-Peier, U. (2022) 'Distance Interpreting in Asylum Proceedings' in UNHCR and Pöllabauer, S. (eds.) *Handbook for Interpreters in Asylum Procedures,* 2nd and revised edition, Berlin: Frank & Timme, pp. 213–39.

Kadrić, M. (2019) *Gerichts- und Behördendolmetschen: Prozessrechtliche und translatorische Perspektiven*. Wien: Facultas Verlags- und Buchhandels AG.

Kadrić, M. (2020) 'Legal Interpreting and Social Discourse' in Ji, M. and Laviosa, S. (eds.) *The Oxford Handbook of Translation and Social Practices*. Oxford: Oxford University Press, pp. 500–20.

Raven, B.H. (1965) 'Social Influence and Power' in Steiner, I.D. and Fishbein, M. (eds.) *Current Studies in Social Psychology*. New York: Holt, Rinehart and Winston, pp. 371–82.
Raven, B.H. (2008) 'The Bases of Power and the Power/Interaction Model of Interpersonal Influence' *Analyses of Social Issues and Public Policy*, 8(1), pp. 1–22 https://doi.org/10.1111/j.1530-2415.2008.00159.x.
Rudvin, M. (2005) 'Power Behind Discourse and Power in Discourse in Community Interpreting: The Effect of Institutional Power Asymmetry on Interpreter Strategies' *Revista Canaria de Estudios Ingleses*, 51, pp. 159–79.
Wadensjö, C. (1998) *Interpreting as Interaction*. London, New York: Longman.
Watzlawick, P., Beavin, J. and Jackson, D.D. (1967) *Pragmatics of Human Communication: A Study of Interactional Patterns, Pathologies, and Paradoxes*. New York: W. W. Norton & Company Inc.
Habermas, J. (1984) *The Theory of Communicative Action*. Translated by T. McCarthy. Boston: Beacon Press.

Online sources

African Court on Human and Peoples' Rights (n.d.) Available at: https://www.african-court.org/wpafc/ (accessed 25 January 2023).
Court of Justice of the European Union (n.d.) https://curia.europa.eu/jcms/jcms/Jo1_6308 (accessed 25 January 2023).
European Court of Human Rights (n.d.) https://www.echr.coe.int/Pages/home.aspx?p=home (accessed 25 January 2023).
European Parliament (2010) 'Directive 2010/64/EU of the European Parliament and of the Council of 20 October 2010 on the Right to Interpretation and Translation in Criminal Proceedings', Official Journal of the European Union, no. 2010/64/EU.
Inter-American Court of Human Rights (n.d.) https://www.corteidh.or.cr/index.cfm?lang=en (accessed 25 January 2023).
International Court of Justice–Cour Internationale De Justice (n.d.) https://www.icj-cij.org/ (accessed 25 January 2023).
International Criminal Court (n.d.) https://www.icc-cpi.int (accessed 25 January 2023).
Remote Courts Worldwide (n.d.) https://remotecourts.org/ (accessed 25 January 2023).

2 Institutional safeguards of rights

Chapter summary

Fundamental principles such as the equal access to justice for all can only be guaranteed for individuals who do not have sufficient command of the *language of service* if professional interpreting is provided. This chapter provides an overview of the most relevant national and supranational legal guarantees for interpreting, which are the basis for the use of interpreters at courts and public authorities. Although the details of this legal framework fall within the purview of individual states, there are unifying principles in international law, which will be presented here. Furthermore, concepts of dignity in the context of interpreting and *questioning* in legal settings will be discussed. Study activities in this chapter include literature reviews and group discussions regarding the country-specific norms on interpreting services.

2.1 Historical background

Interpreting at courts and public authorities is one of the most frequent and essential tasks of interpreters. It is only through their work that participants to the proceedings who do not have sufficient command of the *language of service* can participate. This has become even more important in recent years due to developments such as increased mobility, migration and refugee movements, as well as technological advances and the transnational communication channels they create.

Therefore, mandatory regulations on the use of interpreters in administrative and judicial proceedings are of great importance. Although the specific form of such standards for criminal, civil and asylum proceedings is generally decided at the national level, there are important principles of international law that set some uniform minimum standards for implementation in national law. Such regulations can be found, for example, in the European Convention on Human Rights or the International Covenant on Civil and Political Rights. The European Union has also issued various directives that define rights such as the right to interpretation

DOI: 10.4324/9781003301585-3

of suspected and accused persons and of victims in criminal proceedings in more detail. In the United States, the use of interpreters is governed by the Court Interpreter Act at federal level. In other countries, such as Australia, regulations are found at the level of states and territories. Depending on the legal system in question, regulations can be based mainly on legal norms, as is the case in most European countries, or primarily on court decisions, as in the Anglo-American sphere, which is dominated by *case law*. More and more countries are improving access to justice by providing court interpreters free of charge – for example, the United States has done so since 1991. Interpreting services are also provided by the state in other parts of the world, such as the European Union and Australia, as part of legal aid.

The right to interpretation is an essential part of the right to a fair trial, as it is referred to in Europe, or 'due process' in the Anglo-American sphere. The right to a fair trial encompasses various principles that a modern constitutional state is obliged to uphold for those subject to the law in any proceedings. These include equal access to justice, the right to be heard in court, the right to receive information about the proceedings and the right to legal assistance. It is of particular importance to safeguard fundamental rights in proceedings in which individuals face the state. This is the case, for example, in criminal proceedings, which must meet the highest standards of the rule of law, especially when the consequence of the sentence can be imprisonment or even a death sentence. However, compliance with fundamental rights is also of vital importance in asylum proceedings, where decisions are made on whether someone is granted protection by the state. Although, of course, the fundamental rights must be guaranteed for any party to proceedings, some individuals have a higher need for protection due to their particular personal situations. This may be the case, for example, for victims of crimes who have to cooperate as witnesses in establishing the truth, but who have been personally seriously affected by the crime. Special attention must be paid to their protection. As a rule, it is the responsibility of the courts to decide whether a person is to be provided support in the form of interpreting services or not.

There are, of course, differences in the way individual countries implement this right. Such differences may concern the types of cases where interpreters are used, who pays for them and how extensive the interpretation has to be.

The increasing need for interpretation for courts and authorities has increased awareness of the issue, leading to growing political and academic interest. Today, the discussions focus on areas such as interpreting standards, on-site and remote working conditions, training programmes and ethical issues, showing the relevance of court and public service interpreting in both practice and research.

The right to a fair trial and to unimpeded communication in legal proceedings is a challenge shared by the legal and interpreting professions. This overlap became evident on a large scale for the first time during the 1945–1949 Nuremberg trials, where the International Military Tribunal established by the four major Allied countries tried members of the Nazi leadership for war crimes and crimes against humanity. It is widely regarded as the birth of international criminal law, and it was also a milestone in the history of court interpreting, as interpretation had to be provided into multiple languages. Article 25 of the Charter of the International Military Tribunal provided that all court proceedings were to be conducted in English, French and Russian, and in the language of the defendant, which was mostly German. The aim was to ensure a fair trial for the defendants, who should be able to follow the trial and to communicate and defend themselves in their own language. In addition to enabling communication between defendants, lawyers and witnesses, interpretation also allowed the judges and prosecutors from the four countries to communicate clearly.

There was initially some distrust of the new simultaneous interpreting mode, as both the technology and the mode itself were new – previously, consecutive interpreting had been the dominant mode, but with interpretation required into several languages at the same time, that would not have been feasible.

US Chief Prosecutor Robert H. Jackson, who expressed his concerns about the functioning communication before the trial, stated the importance of fair and dispassionate hearings. This call went out to everyone involved in the Tribunal, naturally including the interpreters, for whom this was often a particular challenge, as several of them were themselves victims of the Nazi regime.

The International Military Tribunal at Nuremberg also served as a model for the Tokyo War Crimes Trial, or the International Military Tribunal for the Far East, between 1946 and 1948. Here, Japanese leaders were tried for crimes against humanity and war crimes.

It was not until the 1990s that another international war crimes tribunal was set up. The International Criminal Tribunal for the Former Yugoslavia (ICTY) from 1993 to 2017 was a multilingual court with interpretation into the working languages English and French and the languages of the defendants and witnesses heard in court. The International Criminal Tribunal for Rwanda, which followed the model of the ICTY, and the International Criminal Court in The Hague can also both trace their roots back to the Nuremberg trial.

2.2 International law

This section provides a summary of major provisions designed to guarantee the right of a person involved in administrative or judicial proceedings to be heard in a language that person understands. These provisions are a matter of fundamental rights and serve to ensure fair proceedings and the right to be heard in court. Since communication between courts and authorities and someone speaking a different language can, in practice, only be established by means of interpretating, these provisions imply the right to the involvement of an interpreter and thus also form the basis for the appointment of interpreters by courts and authorities. It should be emphasised that interpretation not only safeguards the rights of the speakers of other languages: the right to a fair trial can be guaranteed for the parties to the proceedings who speak the *language of service* only if smooth communication with, e.g., a foreign-language witness is ensured. The same applies to the state's right to prosecution in criminal proceedings.

The asylum procedure, where decisions have far-reaching implications, should be considered in a similar light. Here, too, interpreting ensures the right of an applicant seeking protection to communicate in her own language on the one hand and the ability of the authority to ensure fair proceedings on the other. This also applies to other administrative procedures, such as the granting of a business licence or a building permit.

The situation is not much different in matters of *civil law*. Interpreting must also be ensured where citizens settle disputes between themselves in civil proceedings before the courts. It is the involvement of an interpreter that gives speakers of other languages access to justice. However, it must be said that the danger of violating fundamental rights is less pronounced in the area of civil proceedings than in criminal or asylum law. Accordingly, some fundamental rights guarantees also primarily concern these latter areas of law.

2.2.1 Supranational guarantees

Supranational legal norms include mainly international conventions such as the European Convention on Human Rights, the International Covenant on Civil and Political Rights, or the Geneva Convention on Refugees. In addition, there are bilateral and multilateral agreements that affect a limited number of countries. In many cases, international agreements have to be transferred into national law in order to be directly applicable. For the legislation described below, many countries have fulfilled this obligation. However, even if this is not the case, the regulation fulfils an important role, functioning as a form of moral guideline.

The law of the European Union is a legal form of its own: In some areas, the EU has full regulatory competence, while in others, the Union and its member states have shared competence. This gives EU law a special legal character, and it is described in its own section below.

The 1950 European Convention on Human Rights is one of the most important legal regulations. More recently, the European Union issued important standards with the 2000 Charter of Fundamental Rights and, specifically for court and *legal interpreting*, the 2010 Directive on the right to interpretation and translation in criminal proceedings. At the national level, these fundamental rights have been formulated as various procedural laws.

2.2.2 European Convention for the Protection of Human Rights and Fundamental Freedoms (ECHR)

The European Convention for the Protection of Human Rights and Fundamental Freedoms (ECHR) is the most important document for the protection of human rights since the Second World War. It was initially created as a reaction to war and fascism, and signed on 4 November 1950. The ECHR, which was concluded for an indefinite period, can be traced back to the Universal Declaration of Human Rights, in which the United Nations drew up a list of fundamental human rights in 1948. While the UN Declaration of Human Rights is non-binding, the rights granted by the ECHR can be enforced before the European Court of Human Rights (ECtHR) in Strasbourg. The *case law* of the ECtHR has contributed significantly to the development of the European system of fundamental rights. Since the ECHR was enacted within the framework of the Council of Europe and almost all European states are members, its jurisdiction extends well beyond the European Union and also includes countries such as Turkey or Russia.

Article 1 of the ECHR guarantees the rights defined in the Convention to everyone within the jurisdiction of the contracting states, i.e. not only to their own citizens. The scope of application of the ECHR is thus limited to the territories of the states concerned, but there are no restrictions in terms of persons it applies to. The fact that everyone is entitled to the same rights – irrespective of citizenship – is further underlined by Article 14 of the ECHR, which expressly prohibits discrimination on the grounds of sex, race, colour, language, religion, etc.

How they ensure that the provisions of the Convention are applied in national law is left to each contracting state. The procedural guarantees of the ECHR apply to all proceedings involving criminal charges and civil claims and obligations. However, administrative proceedings, such as asylum procedures, are not covered. This has been repeatedly confirmed by past ECtHR decisions.

The ECHR contains the following key provisions on interpretation:

> Article 5: Right to liberty and security
>
> . . .
>
> 2. Everyone who is arrested shall be informed promptly, in a language which he understands, of the reasons for his arrest and of any charge against him.
>
> Article 6: Right to a fair trial
>
> 1. In the determination of his civil rights and obligations or of any criminal charge against him, everyone is entitled to a fair and public hearing within a reasonable time by an independent and impartial tribunal established by law. Judgment shall be pronounced publicly but the press and public may be excluded from all or part of the trial in the interests of morals, public order or national security in a democratic society, where the interests of juveniles or the protection of the private life of the parties so require, or to the extent strictly necessary in the opinion of the court in special circumstances where publicity would prejudice the interests of justice.
>
> . . .
>
> (3) Everyone charged with a criminal offence has the following minimum rights:
>
> (a) to be informed promptly, in a language which he understands and in detail, of the nature and cause of the accusation against him;
>
> . . .
>
> (e) to have the free assistance of an interpreter if he cannot understand or speak the language used in court.

It is clear from the wording in Articles 5 and 6 that 'a language which he understands' does not necessarily mandate the use of the person's first language, but of a language the end user speaks. In practice, this may mean the use of one of the official languages of an end user's country of origin, which does not necessarily equate to his first language, or of a language the end user charged with a criminal offence speaks well, or a *lingua franca.*

The European Court of Human Rights has developed a rich and dynamic jurisprudence on Articles 5 and 6 of the ECHR. The Court has a modern understanding of the provisions of the ECHR and interprets Article 6(1) as a comprehensive guarantee of a fair trial. The right to interpretation for people who do not speak the *language of service* is an important basis for ensuring that they, too, have access to justice and are able to participate actively in the proceedings that concern them. Accordingly, the ECtHR has defined the necessary framework conditions for this right in various decisions. Only compliance with them guarantees the right to a fair trial. Most of these decisions concern criminal proceedings, in which the state has a particularly pronounced obligation to protect the defendant's rights.

Thus, the task of ensuring that interpreting, and with it the possibility of participating in the proceedings, is provided falls to the court. It is not sufficient for the court to call in an interpreter when the suspect or defendant requests it. Rather, as soon as there is any indication that the suspect or defendant is not sufficiently proficient in the *language of service,* the court must actively inform them about the possibility of interpreting and then ensure that an interpreter is called in. The court is also responsible for selecting the specific person who will interpret. Along with this, the court also has the obligation to confirm that the interpreter is fundamentally suited for the task. While the ECHR does not specify the appointment process, the quality of the interpretation must be such that it enables the end user concerned to participate actively in the proceedings. All this applies not only during the main hearing, but already in the pre-trial proceedings.

The interpretation must always be free of charge for the person suspected or accused of a crime. The interpreter must therefore be paid by the state. This applies regardless of whether the suspect is ultimately convicted or not. The ECHR specifically refers to interpreters, not translators. Accordingly, the ECtHR also recognises that this primarily includes oral interpretation. However, according to the Court's decisions, the translation of individual documents or the communication of their contents to the suspect or defendant are also covered by the rights in Article 6. The deciding factor here is again the fundamental requirement that suspects or defendants must be able to participate actively in the proceedings and defend themselves. Where this is only possible if they are aware of the contents of certain documents, these must be brought to their attention in a language they understand.

The International Criminal Tribunal for the former Yugoslavia (ICTY), which existed from 1993 to 2017 and was set up as a multilingual court with English and French as working languages, is an example of the implementation of the ECHR's requirements. Each person accused at the ICTY had the right to use a language familiar to them, so the languages Bosnian/Croatian/Serbian were regularly used; other languages were also used when necessary, such as Albanian in the trial of Slobodan Milošević or Dutch in the Srebrenica trial.

The need for interpreting and translation at the ICTY went far beyond the high-profile trials of the main defendants. At the beginning of this century, between 500 and 600 witnesses per year from around 25 countries were heard in the trials of the Hague Tribunal. All of these witnesses were contacted in advance in their home countries. This procedure, which set new standards in victim protection, caused an enormous demand for translation and interpreting services.

The translators and interpreters working in The Hague were among the best in their profession. This was necessary because the Court wanted to be sure that the statements of the witnesses would reach the court unaltered in order to determine the truth and clarify the facts of the case. The accuseds, in turn, had the guarantee that their statements would be interpreted without alteration into the languages of the trial and, conversely, that the Court's communications would be conveyed to them correctly every time.

In Rwanda in 1994, at least 800,000 people were killed in just 100 days. The UN Security Council then established the International Criminal Tribunal for Rwanda (ICTR). The Tribunal carried out its work from 1995 to 2015 in Arusha, Tanzania, and it became the first international criminal court to issue convictions for genocide. The rules of procedure were based on those of the ICTY. Here, too, the statute provided that each accused 'shall be informed promptly and in detail in a language which he or she understands, of the nature and cause of the charge against him'. The interpretation practice of the ICTR has sometimes been criticised in literature for its lack of quality and technical resources.

2.2.3 International Covenant on Civil and Political Rights (ICCPR)

This international covenant is a treaty under international law that was adopted by the UN General Assembly in 1966 and entered into force in 1976. Together with the Universal Declaration of Human Rights, the International Covenant on Economic, Social and Cultural Rights (ICESCR) and several optional protocols, the Covenant forms the International Bill of Human Rights. Currently, 173 states are parties to the Covenant, and six other states have signed but not ratified the treaty.

The Covenant aims to secure individual civil and political rights, such as the right to life and physical integrity, the right to liberty and security of person, freedom of religion or freedom of expression. The States Parties undertake to implement the rights laid out in the Covenant, although it should be noted that declarations and reservations may apply, as some states are not prepared to implement individual provisions of the Covenant because of national laws. In this case, a state may declare a reservation, which enables that state to become a party to the Covenant but not be bound by certain provisions.

The United Nations Human Rights Committee is responsible for monitoring compliance. The parties to the Covenant must regularly report to the Committee on the implementation of the rights of the Covenant in national legislation. If a state violates its obligations under the Covenant, the Committee can issue recommendations for improvement to the state. However, these recommendations are not legally binding. In general, there is no possibility for individuals to sue for the rights under the Covenant.

The ICCPR contains the right to a fair trial in Article 14. Paragraph 1 contains the fundamental provisions for this right, such as that all persons are equal before the courts and tribunals and that, if criminal charges or civil claims are brought against them, they are entitled to a fair and public hearing by a competent, independent and impartial tribunal established by law. Article 14 also includes the presumption of innocence until proven guilty, as well as the right to have a conviction reviewed by a higher tribunal. Paragraph 3 includes various minimum guarantees for criminal proceedings. Two of these provisions are relevant to interpreting:

> 3. In the determination of any criminal charge against him, everyone shall be entitled to the following minimum guarantees, in full equality:
>
> (a) To be informed promptly and in detail in a language which he understands of the nature and cause of the charge against him;
>
> (. . .)
>
> (f) To have the free assistance of an interpreter if he cannot understand or speak the language used in court (. . .)

Just as with the ECHR, these are minimum requirements that states must meet, meaning that they may at any time grant rights that exceed these requirements. The Human Rights Committee has issued few statements that would clarify the concrete form of these rights. Therefore, it is less clear than Article 6 of the ECHR, on which there is comprehensive *case law* of the ECtHR, as mentioned above. Generally speaking, it can be said that the provision of an interpreter is intended to enable the end user concerned to participate actively in the proceedings. Questions such as the timing and duration of the appointment, the scope of the interpretation and the interpreter's qualifications should be determined based on this standard.

2.2.4 Geneva Convention Relating to the Status of Refugees

The Geneva Refugee Convention remains the most important international document for the protection of refugees. It was adopted on 28 July 1951 at a UN special conference to determine the legal status of refugees, and entered into force on 22 April 1954. The Convention protects persons who are persecuted for reasons of race, religion, nationality, membership of a particular social group or political opinion. The Convention guarantees these people protection and defines their rights and obligations in the contracting states. The original scope of the Refugee Convention was designed for European refugees after the Second World War, but the scope was extended with a 1967 Protocol that removed the geographic and time limits. To date, 149 states have acceded to the Convention.

Article 16 of the Convention guarantees refugees free access to the courts and the same treatment as nationals in all matters pertaining to access to the courts. The UN High Commissioner for Refugees (UNHCR) monitors the application of the Convention.

Figure 2.1 Major international safeguards of rights

This review shows that the rules of the international criminal courts consistently provide for suspects to be informed promptly of the charges against them and of their rights. In the case of suspects and accused persons who do not speak the *language of service*, there is a risk that this information will be delayed due to communication difficulties and the frequent lack of interpreters on site, and thus treated unequally. The use of modern technology such as video conferencing helps to protect the rights of suspects and accused persons who do not speak the *language of service* and to inform them of their rights without significant delay in their first language or in a language they understand.

2.3 Law of the European Union

At the Nice European Council in December 2000, the European Union proclaimed its own human rights document, the Charter of Fundamental Rights of the European Union. The Charter is now legally binding and applies where EU law applies. Its Article 1 is slightly modified version of the introductory sentences of the German Basic Law: 'Human dignity is inviolable. It must be respected and protected.'

Around the turn of the millennium, the European Union increasingly began harmonising criminal and *civil law*, for which it was successively given new competences. In this context, the European Union also considered matters of communication in the public sphere in depth. The European Commission conducted a broad discussion process with scholars and practitioners of law and of interpreting and translation over several years; this work resulted in the central European document on court interpreting, the 2010 Directive on the right to interpretation and translation in criminal proceedings. It was followed by a number of further Directives on matters of criminal law and asylum law in which interpretation plays a role. We will briefly discuss the Charter of Fundamental Rights and the relevant directives below.

2.3.1 *European Charter of Fundamental Rights (CFR)*

The Charter of Fundamental Rights applies to the European institutions and bodies and to the Member States where they apply EU law. The Charter encompasses civil, political, economic and social rights, and organises them in six chapters titled Dignity, Freedoms, Equality, Solidarity, Citizens' rights, and Justice. The legal guarantees relevant to equitable communication can be found in Articles 21, 22, 47 and 48.

Article 21(1) prohibits discrimination based, in particular, on sex, race, colour, ethnic or social origin, genetic features, language, religion or belief, political or any other opinion, membership of a national minority, property, birth, disability, age or sexual orientation. Article 22 contains the general declaration that the Union shall respects cultural, religious and linguistic diversity.

Article 47 grants everyone the right to an effective remedy and to a fair trial. The provision relevant to the field of interpretation reads:

> [E]veryone is entitled to a fair and public hearing within a reasonable time by an independent and impartial tribunal previously established by law. Everyone shall have the possibility of being advised, defended and represented.

Here, the meaning of Article 47 corresponds to that of Article 6 of the ECHR. There, too, the principle of a fair trial is of decisive relevance to the use of interpreters. This is also referred to in Article 48 (2), which reads

Respect for the rights of the defence of anyone who has been charged shall be guaranteed.

This corresponds to Article 6(3) of the ECHR and thus also encompasses the previously mentioned right of an accused person to the assistance of an interpreter should they not be sufficiently proficient in the *language of service*. The *case law* of the European Court of Human Rights on the interpretation of fundamental rights is relevant for the European Court of Justice with its seat in Luxembourg.

2.3.2 *Directives of the European Parliament and European Council*

2.3.2.1 *Directive 2010/64/EC: Interpreting and translation directive*

The European Union was given competences to legislate matters related to criminal law only at a fairly late stage, with the Treaty of Lisbon in 2007. These competences continue to be very limited and are primarily aimed at harmonising certain minimum standards in procedural rights. After several legislative initiatives by the Commission and individual Member States, the European Council and Parliament adopted the Directive on the Right to Interpretation and Translation in Criminal Proceedings (Directive 2010/64/EU). Directive 2010/64/EU was the first legal act adopted by the Union in the field criminal procedure law. This shows how important the legislators consider interpretation for the quality of criminal proceedings. The background to the Directive is the European Union's endeavour to achieve mutual recognition of decisions in criminal matters. A prerequisite for this is fundamental trust of the member states in each other's legal systems as well as proper compliance with and application of rules in criminal law. Reference is made to Art 6 ECHR, the Charter of Fundamental Rights and the relevant decisions of the ECtHR, and it is stated that the level of protection of the persons concerned should never fall below those standards.

The recitals of the Directive elaborate on the importance of translation and interpretation by referring to the Union's work since the Tampere European Council in 1999, and in particular to the Convention on Human Rights and the Charter of Fundamental Rights of the European Union. The text of the Directive itself is short; it is worth reading the recitals that precede it. They summarise the professional discussion on court interpreting at the beginning of this century. The requirements of the Directive are minimum rules. Therefore, the member states are free to create additional legal standards that serve the aims of the Directive, first and foremost the protection of the rights of accused persons.

The Directive requires member states to provide all suspected or accused persons who do not speak or understand the *language of service* with sufficient quality interpretation during criminal proceedings – not only during the main hearing, but also for any interim hearings, police *questioning* and communication with their legal counsel (Article 2).

It also establishes a right to a written translation of all documents essential to the defence in order to enable defendants to exercise their right of defence so as to ensure a fair trial. These essential documents include, by explicit reference, any decision restricting liberty, any charge or indictment, and any judgment. This right can only be waived under special conditions. However, the Directive provides for the possibility of an oral translation or oral summary of such documents instead of a written translation if this does not prejudice the fairness of the proceedings (Article 3).

With regard to both oral interpretation and written translation, Member States must ensure that the persons concerned are able to challenge a decision not to provide interpretation or translation services, and to complain if the quality of these services is not sufficient (Article 2(5) and Article 3(5)).

The Directive also addresses the quality of interpretation and translation (Article 5) and requires Member States to endeavour to establish one or more registers of independent interpreters and translators appropriately qualified for this task (Article 5). Finally, it also addresses the training of judicial staff in translation matters (Article 6).

The Directive includes the important clarification that it is the state's task to determine whether there is a need for interpretation, rather than the suspect having to ask for interpretation. According to Article 2(4), the Member States of the European Union must establish a procedure or mechanism to ascertain whether suspected or accused persons understand the *language of service* and whether they need interpretation – and by extension probably also for which language.

An important element of the Directive is that interpretation is guaranteed free of charge also for the communication between the accused and his legal counsel

(Article 4). The Directive builds on the modern understanding that the state must provide suspects who do not speak the *language of service* with interpretation services free of charge for communication with their legal counsel, not only in the case of legal aid or an appointed counsel, but also with a freely chosen lawyer. Only such an understanding guarantees speakers of other languages the same access to justice as persons who speak the *language of service*. A fair trial can hardly be guaranteed without ensuring communication between the suspected person and his defence, even in the run-up to a court hearing.

Article 2(6) of the Directive explicitly allows for the use of video interpretation or other technology-assisted translation services: 'Where appropriate, communication technology, such as videoconferencing, telephone or the Internet may be used, unless the physical presence of the interpreter is required in order to safeguard the fairness of the proceedings.' Recital 28 elaborates that the competent authorities may use tools that are being developed in the context of European e-Justice, such as information on courts with videoconferencing equipment or manuals.

The long-discussed mandatory audio or video recording of all interpreted hearings and negotiations was ultimately not included in the Directive. Its introduction is therefore left to the discretion of the individual member states.

As many member states delayed implementing the Directive, the Commission did not produce its mandated report on the effects of the Directive until 2018. Issues with implementation were noted in several countries, particularly with regard to communication between suspected or accused persons and their legal counsel, translation of essential documents, and the costs of interpretation and translation. The Commission stated that it would issue warnings and even initiate infringement proceedings where necessary. At the same time, the Commission concluded that overall, the Directive had already provided the EU added value by raising the level of protection of citizens involved in criminal proceedings, especially in some Member States where the right to translation and interpretation had not previously existed. The Commission proposed not to revise the Directive for the time being, but to improve its application in practice.

The Directive on the right to interpretation and translation in criminal proceedings was only the first of six Directives harmonising procedural rights in criminal proceedings in the EU. Interpreting and translation play a recurring role in these Directives. Two of them are discussed below.

2.3.3 *Other relevant Directives of the European Union*

2.3.3.1 *Criminal Law*

2.3.3.1.1 DIRECTIVE 2012/29/EU

The 2012 Directive establishing minimum standards on the rights, support and protection of victims of crime and replacing Council Framework Decision 2001/220/JHA complements the Interpreting Directive with regard to the rights of persons involved in criminal proceedings to interpretation and translation services. While the Interpreting Directive is intended to safeguard the rights of the accused, the Victim Protection Directive stipulates the rights of the victims of crime. According to Article 7 of this Directive, victims who do not know the *language of service* must be provided with interpretation in accordance with their role in the relevant criminal justice system on request and free of charge. This must be the case at least during any interviews or *questioning* of the victim by investigative and judicial authorities (including police *questioning*). Even when reporting a crime, the victim must be able to do so in a language they understand (Article 5). Overall, victims must be enabled to participate actively in court hearings and any necessary interim hearings. Written translations are also to be provided to victims free of charge upon request if the information is essential for the exercise of their rights. Such essential documents include at least any decision ending the criminal proceedings, and upon the victim's request, reasons or a brief summary of reasons for the decision (except in the case of a jury decision). Victims can also submit a request for a document to be considered as essential. Here, too, an oral translation can be provided as an alternative to a written one.

Like the Interpreting Directive, Article 7(2) provides for distance interpretation: '(2) without prejudice to the rights of the defence and in accordance with rules of judicial discretion, communication technology such as videoconferencing, telephone or internet may be used, unless the physical presence of the interpreter is required in order for the victims to properly exercise their rights or to understand the proceedings.'

2.3.3.1.2 DIRECTIVE 2012/13/EU

The Directive on the right to information in criminal proceedings (Directive 2012/13/EU) sets rules for the information that must be given to suspects and accused persons in criminal proceedings. Article 3 of the Directive lists the rights they must be informed of, which includes information about the right to interpretation and translation. Article 4(5) requires that suspects or accused persons receive a written explanation of their rights ('Letter of Rights') in a language they understand. If the Letter of Rights is not available in the appropriate language, it may be replaced by an oral explanation in a language the suspect or accused person understands. However, a Letter of Rights in a language they understand must be provided without undue delay.

2.3.3.2 Asylum and aliens law

Two EU Directives are of interest to us regarding the procedure before the asylum and aliens authorities: Directive 2013/32/EU on common procedures for granting and withdrawing international protection (recast) and Directive 2013/33/EU laying down standards for the reception of applicants for international protection (recast).

2.3.3.2.1 DIRECTIVE 2013/32/EU

This Directive contains several references to the necessity of interpretation. For example, Article 12 provides that all applicants shall be informed, in a language they understand or are reasonably supposed to understand, of the procedure to be followed and of their rights and obligations during the procedure, as well as of the possible consequences of not complying with their obligations and not cooperating with the authorities. To this end, Member States are to use the service of an interpreter where necessary. The Directive assumes that interpretation is necessary when 'appropriate communication cannot be ensured without such services'. The costs for the interpreter must always be borne by the public authorities. For the personal interview, which is an important part of the asylum procedure, the Directive provides in Article 15 that Member States must select an interpreter who is 'able to ensure appropriate communication between the applicant and the person who conducts the interview'. The Directive makes detailed provisions here:

> The communication shall take place in the language preferred by the applicant unless there is another language which he or she understands and in which he or she is able to communicate clearly. Wherever possible, Member States shall provide an interpreter of the same sex if the applicant so requests, unless the determining authority has reasons to believe that such a request is based on grounds which are not related to difficulties on the part of the applicant to present the grounds of his or her application in a comprehensive manner.

Article 17 grants applicants the right to comment or provide clarification orally and/or in writing regarding any mistranslations or misconceptions appearing in the report or transcript. To this end, Member States must ensure that the applicant is fully informed of the content of the report, if necessary through interpretation.

2.3.3.2.2 DIRECTIVE 2013/33/EU

The second relevant document on the asylum procedure provides in Article 5 that applicants must be provided with certain information on established benefits and obligations. Paragraph 2 establishes that this must be done in a language that the applicant understands or is reasonably supposed to understand. If an applicant is detained, they must be informed, in the same manner, of the reasons for detention and the procedure for challenging the detention order, as well as of the possibility to request free legal assistance and representation (Article 9). Article 10 provides that applicants in detention be systematically provided with information on the rules applied in the facility and that their rights and obligations be explained to them in a language they understand or are reasonably supposed to understand.

2.3.3.3 Other provisions

In addition to the areas of criminal and asylum law, in which interpreting services are of crucial importance, there are also provisions in EU Directives governing the use of interpreters in other areas of law. For example, Directive 2011/36/EU on preventing and combating trafficking in human beings and protecting its victims stipulates in Article 11 that victims of trafficking must be provided with various assistance and support measures, and explicitly mentions translation and interpreting services. Similar provisions are contained in Directive 2004/81/EC, which regulates the residence of victims of trafficking. According to Article 7, the affected persons must be given various support services, and here, too, interpretation services are emphasised: 'Member States shall provide the third-country nationals concerned, where appropriate, with translation and interpreting services.'

2.4 Concepts of dignity in the context of communication in legal settings

As we have seen, the ability to communicate in a language one understands in legal settings is a matter of access to justice and a fair trial. However, it is also a matter of dignity. As the facilitators of that communication, interpreters have a big responsibility not only to have the skill and competence to understand what is being said and the strategies to express that in another language, they also need to understand and follow professional ethics.

Rules of professional conduct provide a framework that describes the behaviour expected of a member of a certain profession, lays out possible actions and defines their responsibilities. These responsibilities include those towards one's colleagues, clients and the profession and its image, but they also refer to our attitudes and what we see as our responsibility, from a moral or ethical point of view. Court interpreting associations around the world have developed codes of ethics that usually lay out the general responsibilities and roles of interpreters, based on the codes of conduct of other professions, empirical research and legal regulations.

Codes of ethics for interpreting are frequently grounded in law and the general understanding that democratic societies have of fundamental rights such as dignity and equal treatment as moral rights, and this is reflected in particular in areas where interpreting may affect a person's liberty, safety, security and integrity, such as in asylum proceedings, in family law or in criminal law. The concepts of human dignity, liberty and integrity are closely interlinked.

Dignity was long mainly an ethical and philosophical concept, but it has found its way into law – such as the German Basic Law's statement about the inviolability of human dignity, which is also reflected in the EU Charter of Fundamental Rights, as discussed above. Perhaps as a learning from the darkest chapters of the 20th century, the concept of dignity and of protecting groups that particularly need it, such as children, the elderly, people with illnesses and disabilities, has become increasingly important in law, e.g. when regulating asylum procedures or setting standards of care for nursing homes. It is a way of making law and institutions more suited to the people they serve. Dignity is an inherent value of all humans. According to Article 1 of the Charter of Fundamental Rights of the European Union, human dignity is inviolable. This means that it must be respected and protected. This fundamental provision emphasises the inalienable rights of and respect due to every individual by virtue of their very existence. Respect for human dignity is thus a central principle for the protection and promotion of the rights and freedoms of all people in the European Union. In principle, this applies to the entire democratic world.

This concept of dignity as a legal and moral imperative also helps us set guidelines for interpreting in legal settings. It may be a legal requirement, such as in court or asylum proceedings, where it is derived from international treaties, but considering dignity when interpreting in legal settings, be they in court or with lawyers or notaries, can also guide the individual interpreter in decision-making and professional organisations in establishing codes of conduct.

We can draw on literature from the fields of ethics and philosophy, where e.g. the philosopher Peter Bieri (2013) writes that every adult strives for autonomy and self-determination, and that being able to act in a self-determined way is an important part of dignity. Other aspects of dignity mentioned in his book *Human Dignity: A Way of Living* include dignity of encounter, respect for intimacy, truthfulness, self-respect, moral integrity, a sense of what matters and the acceptance of finitude. All of these can apply to interpreted situations, especially in the legal sphere. Asylum applications where the most intimate details must be disclosed, testifying as a witness of sexual assault, or matters of family law may all affect the autonomy or the respect for intimacy of those involved. Their dignity, especially in terms of intimacy, must be protected by the courts as well as by the interpreters. The interpreter's responsibility is to help ensure that they are not humiliated. Dignity of encounter is another important aspect in this regard. As Bieri writes, every person has the right and the desire to be treated as equal in an encounter and to have agency. This is violated if someone is manipulated, put on display or treated like a number. Pity, too, can be seen as humiliating or condescending, and speaking about someone as if they were not there is particularly hurtful, as it denies them agency and removes them from the communication – in the case of interpreted communication often completely, as they will not understand what is being said about them. As a part of the communicative situation, and as the person who usually is the one enabling communication in the first place, the interpreter plays a crucial role in ensuring the dignity and agency of everyone involved are respected.

The interpreter's work is always guided by professional codes of ethics, regardless of the setting. In court and public service interpreting, there may be additional legal regulations or institutional guidelines or codes of conduct that inform her behaviour and interpreting strategies, but the principles central to the interpreting profession are always the same: truthfulness, objectivity, transparency, confidentiality and, above all, the impartial – or multipartial – enabling of communication for all participants. The interpreter acts in the interests of others, and does so in an unbiased way that respects the dignity and right of everyone involved to express themselves and understand others. In legal and administrative settings in general, and in *questioning* situations in particular, the objective is to establish the truth and the facts of the case. This holds true for preliminary investigations, criminal proceedings, civil litigation and administrative proceedings alike, e.g. when applying for a permit that requires a hearing. The responsibility of the interpreter is to aid this by conveying what has been said without censoring or judging morally or legally. This requires maintaining a personal distance from the matter at hand.

Depending on the situation, the interpretation may focus on conveying the content completely and correctly in a way that ensures comprehension or it may, in addition to completeness and correctness, maintain the style, language register and even self-corrections and hesitations of the speaker, as will be discussed below.

Codes of ethics of professional organisations and legal regulations may also govern how to handle conflicts of interest, i.e. situations where the interpreter has a personal connection to one of the parties or financial, business or other interest in the outcome of the proceedings. Although there may be exceptions to this in private situations, such as when assisting a relative in purchasing a flat, transparency and full disclosure of interests is important in such cases as well. Transparency is also necessary when correcting mistakes: an interpreting mistake can have far-reaching consequences, and should be corrected immediately upon noticing in a way that is transparent for all parties, e.g. by the interpreter referring to themself in third person, gesturing for a pause in the dialogue, asking for help to solve a still-unsolved language issue. Confidentiality is another principle of interpreting codes that is frequently also governed by legal regulations, i.e. treating any information acquired in the course of an assignment as strictly confidential. Transparency, confidentiality and truthfulness allow the interpreter to enable communication between parties with often conflicting interests without favouring one side or the other.

Study activities

- *Legal system*
    - Identify the legal systems that are relevant to your professional role as an interpreter.
    - What are the national legal sources that regulate the work of interpreters in your country? Distinguish between different types of legal sources.
    - Read the legal sources related to interpreting in your country and discuss whether, in your opinion, they are sufficient for you to perform your duties as an interpreter.
    - Do these legal sources also consider recognised minority languages in your country?

- *Rights of defendants in criminal proceedings*
  - List the minimum rights afforded to defendants in criminal proceedings in relation to interpretation and translation services in your country.
  - Discuss the implications of these minimum rights for both defendants and interpreters.
  - Discuss a real or hypothetical case where these minimum rights would be applicable and how they would affect the outcome.
  - Compare and contrast the rights of defendants in criminal proceedings in your country with those in the country (or countries) of your other working language(s), focusing on interpretation and translation services.
  - Assess the adequacy of the rights provided to defendants in criminal proceedings in your country, particularly in relation to interpretation and translation services. Are they sufficient? Why or why not?
- *Ethical issues*
  - Analyse the chapters from the Charter, in particular how the Charter covers the areas of dignity and equality. Then focus on Articles 21, 22, 47 and 48 to understand the legal guarantees for fair communication. Discuss how these provisions might affect the challenges and opportunities for interpreters.
  - Imagine you are the interpreter in a criminal case and you overhear a conversation between two witnesses who agree to make false statements against the defendant. You are the only one who knows about this agreement. What ethical considerations and responsibilities could you take into account? Discuss a course of action that is consistent with the ethical principles of *multipartiality*, confidentiality and integrity. Discuss possible consequences and think about how your decisions could affect the integrity of the criminal proceedings.

By following this structure, learners can engage with the material on multiple cognitive levels, from basic recall to critical evaluation.

Sources and further reading

Legal sources:

- European Convention on Human Rights: https://echr.coe.int/Pages/home.aspx?p=basictexts/convention
- International Covenant on Civil and Political Rights: https://www.ohchr.org/sites/default/files/ccpr.pdf

- The 1951 Refugee Convention: https://www.unhcr.org/media/28185
- Charter of Fundamental Rights of the European Union: https://eur-lex.europa.eu/legal-content/EN/TXT/?uri=CELEX:12012P/TXT
- Directive 2010/64/EU of the European Parliament and of the Council of 20 October 2010 on the right to interpretation and translation in criminal proceedings: https://eur-lex.europa.eu/legal-content/EN/ALL/?uri=celex%3A32010L0064
- Directive 2012/29/EU of the European Parliament and of the Council of 25 October 2012 establishing minimum standards on the rights, support and protection of victims of crime, and replacing Council Framework Decision 2001/220/JHA: https://eur-lex.europa.eu/legal-content/EN/TXT/?uri=CELEX%3A32012L0029&qid=1686641139175
- Directive 2012/13/EU of the European Parliament and of the Council of 22 May 2012 on the right to information in criminal proceedings: https://eur-lex.europa.eu/legal-content/EN/TXT/?uri=CELEX%3A32012L0013
- Directive 2013/32/EU of the European Parliament and of the Council of 26 June 2013 on common procedures for granting and withdrawing international protection (recast): https://eur-lex.europa.eu/legal-content/EN/TXT/?uri=celex%3A32013L0032
- Directive 2013/33/EU of the European Parliament and of the Council of 26 June 2013 laying down standards for the reception of applicants for international protection (recast): https://eur-lex.europa.eu/legal-content/EN/TXT/?uri=celex%3A32013L0033
- Directive 2011/36/EU of the European Parliament and of the Council of 5 April 2011 on preventing and combating trafficking in human beings and protecting its victims, and replacing Council Framework Decision 2002/629/JHA: https://eur-lex.europa.eu/legal-content/EN/ALL/?uri=CELEX%3A32011L0036
- Council Directive 2004/81/EC of 29 April 2004 on the residence permit issued to third-country nationals who are victims of trafficking in human beings or who have been the subject of an action to facilitate illegal immigration, who cooperate with the competent authorities: https://eur-lex.europa.eu/legal-content/EN/ALL/?uri=celex%3A32004L0081

Important decisions of the ECtHR:

- Leudicke, Belkacem and Koç v Germany, http://hudoc.echr.coe.int/eng#{%22itemid%22:[%22001-57530%22]}
- Protopapa v Turkey, https://hudoc.echr.coe.int/fre#{%22itemid%22:[%22001-22707%22
- Kamasinski v Austria, https://hudoc.echr.coe.int/eng#{%22itemid%22:[%22001-57614%22
- Vizgirda v Slovenia, https://hudoc.echr.coe.int/fre#{%22itemid%22:[%22001-185306%22

Further literature

Bieri, P. (2013) *Eine Art zu leben: Über die Vielfalt menschlicher Würde*. München: Hanser.
Clooney, A. and Webb, P. (2020) *The Right to a Fair Trial in International Law*. Oxford: Oxford University Press.
Cras, S. and de Matteis, L. (2010) 'The Directive on the Right to Interpretation and Translation in Criminal Proceedings: Genesis and Description' *The European Criminal Law Associations' Forum*, 4, pp. 153–62.
Dingfelder Stone, J. H. (2018) 'The Right to an Interpreter' in Dingfelder Stone, J. H. (Ed.) *Court Interpreters and Fair Trials*. Cham: Palgrave Macmillan, pp. 9–51.
Gaiba, F. (1998) *The Origins of Simultaneous Interpretation: The Nuremberg Trial*. Ottawa: University Press.
Haas, N. (2011) *Dolmetschen am Ruanda-Tribunal*. Berlin: Lang.
Kadrić, M. (2019) *Gerichts- und Behördendolmetschen: Prozessrechtliche und translatorische Perspektiven*. Wien: Facultas Verlags- und Buchhandels AG.
Vogiatzis, N. (2022) 'Interpreting the Right to Interpretation under Article 6 (3) (e) ECHR: A Cautious Evolution in the Jurisprudence of the European Court of Human Rights?' *Human Rights Law Review*, 22, pp. 1–25.

3 Interpreting as part of communication in legal settings and at public authorities

Chapter summary

This chapter introduces the reader to fundamental concepts of translatorial action in legal settings. We discuss the performativity of language in a legal context and focus particularly on the *questioning* situation from a transdisciplinary perspective that centres legal communication and cooperativity. We explore modes of interpreting that are used in legal settings and have an impact on the interaction. We introduce different forms of technology-supported communication used in the legal context. Study activities in this chapter include group discussions and individual reflections on cooperativity and translatorial action.

3.1 Legal systems and forms of communication

Translatorial action is guided by an overarching goal. From a holistic perspective, the aim of interpreting is to enable all participants to communicate successfully with each other, regardless of their position or function. It is essential for interpreting to ensure full understanding on all sides. The top priority is to establish communication, guided by the principle of function-in-situation.

There is a wide variety of communicative situations in the legal system. Interpreters are used in all legal systems to support communication. Globally, there are two main widely used legal systems: the (codified) continental European and the (uncodified) Anglo Saxon one. Most of continental Europe, as well as South America and parts of Asia and Africa use the former, which is also referred to as civil law, while the Anglo-American sphere uses the latter, called common law. These two systems have fundamental differences, although there has been some convergence in recent years, not least due to advancing globalisation.

In civil law, which goes back to Roman law, codified legal norms represent the highest legal authority. The legislature of a country issues written norms that prescribe rules for the conduct of those subject to the law in an abstract manner. The courts then apply these laws to individual cases in judicial or administrative

DOI: 10.4324/9781003301585-4

proceedings. Once the facts of a case have been determined, the court applies the corresponding law and considers the case in this light. Accordingly, the role of judges is to apply the laws. In contrast, common law countries very rarely have codified laws. The main source of law in this system are previous decisions by the courts, which serve as precedents for later proceedings. This is referred to as *case law*. A court can only deviate from previously made decisions under certain circumstances. Such a change in *case law* is called overruling. Thus, the role of judges in this system is to shape and develop the law.

Nevertheless, there are certain overlaps between these two systems. On the one hand, an increasing codification of legal norms can be seen in common law countries, which means that the role of judges in shaping the law is losing some of its importance. On the other hand, in civil law countries, decisions by appellate courts also have a significance that goes beyond the case in question, as the written laws are often so general and abstract that an interpretation of the legal text by the judiciary is required. Although precedents do not have a binding effect, they nevertheless guide subsequent decisions.

Along with these differences in the shaping of law, procedural requirements also differ significantly between these two systems. In civil law, the inquisitorial system is applied. The court is responsible for conducting the proceedings and determining the facts of the case. Accordingly, it is primarily the court that takes evidence and questions persons during the trial. There are only a few rules regarding the assessment of evidence which provide the framework for how the court is to interpret and evaluate statements and evidence. In contrast, common law countries follow the *adversarial system*. Here, it is increasingly up to the parties to determine the content of the trial, for example by naming witnesses, who are primarily questioned by the parties or their representatives. The court's role is more to ensure compliance with procedure. Common law has complex rules for considering evidence. In general, the process in the civil law system focuses more on the written word, whereas in common law systems, the proceedings, which are conducted orally, have the highest priority. *Legal interpreting* is largely established and standardised in both the continental European and the Anglo-American legal systems. While the approach in the continental European legal tradition is fundamentally system-oriented, common law has a strongly adversarial approach. The requirements for legal interpreters can differ depending on the legal tradition or system.

In civil law, which is applied in large parts of mainland Europe, procedural rules serve as a basis for *questioning*. All procedural steps and the entire course of the hearing are recorded in writing. Taking evidence through *questioning* is one of several forms of evidence. The basis for the decision is often a written transcript of the interpretation, so without a complete interpretation it is not possible to gain a full view of what was said. Decisions of the European Court of Human Rights, however, permit summarised interpretations in court. In these decisions, interpreters are considered expert witnesses at the same time, with the expectation that they still ensure complete communication, and add explanations on the cultural background or specific facts where necessary. How exactly this is to be accomplished may be determined by each country, but the essence is that interpreters must convey all essential parts of the proceedings in full including any emphasis or redundancies. In any case, *questioning* must be interpreted in its entirety.

In the Anglo-American legal sphere, legal and public service interpreting has also been given a great deal of attention. In North America, for example, interpreters are present in the courtroom throughout the entire proceedings.

The judge or other legal actors might address the interpreter rather than the person being questioned, or interpreters might interrupt or instruct the *person being questioned* to respond. If the interpreter asks clarifying questions, this can influence the dynamics in the triad. Through this process, interpreters may influence the proceedings, which may sometimes be in line with the goal of one of the parties to the proceedings, but can change their course considerably. This is notable as the legal rules for interpreting in the courtroom focus mainly on linguistic issues and less on extra-linguistic factors.

3.2 (Legal) language as a means of communication and action

Language is a versatile medium. In law, language can function as a means of communication or as an action, or speech act. Language in the legal setting is normative and performative at the same time; it guides the behaviour of the participants in the proceedings and performs legal actions.

The right to be heard is a central element of a fair trial; unimpeded communication is a basic prerequisite for successful legal proceedings. Awareness of the importance of high-quality interpreting and translation has increased in recent decades. Interpreting ensures equality of arms and opportunities and thus a fair trial that enables all parties to exercise their rights without regard to origin or language. The verbal presentation of facts plays a major role in proceedings in court and with public authorities. The examination of witnesses and, in particular, parties should allow the reconstruction of the facts of the case. Language, or interpretation, as a medium is therefore central to the gathering of evidence.

Language as a verbal means of communication is used in interaction with the primary function of conveying an intended piece of information to an end user. In this process, the speaker's norms, conventions and culturally conditioned ideas as well as individual characteristics are incorporated into the text. The reception of the text is also influenced by social and individual characteristics. These characteristics include elements and meanings that do not need to be expressed linguistically, but are implicitly understood as shared prior knowledge. Language as an element of a culture and the conventional means of communication is filled with assumptions, and communicators interpret these background assumptions through the thought patterns of their own language and culture.

It is obvious that language is only one of several aspects of communication – especially of interpreted communication – and that the important thing about communication is understanding. Consider how differently supposedly 'universal' terms can be interpreted: People from different cultures, but often also people with a shared culture, imbue terms like 'court', 'police' or '*questioning*' with different meanings. Even people involved in the same court proceedings are so deeply influenced by their own (sub-)culture that they do not consciously perceive their cultural assumptions and are not aware that they use them in communication. These individual, culturally influenced characteristics are expressed in language as well as in the way we think, in our behavioural patterns and values, but also in non-verbal communication or how we perceive space and time. These characteristics are functionally linked to each other and only gain significance in the overall context.

When different languages are used in a communicative situation, it may be the case that the communicating parties do not have the same background assumptions. The languages they speak – and which can range from standard language to dialects or lexically limited language (as in the case of a *lingua franca*) – draw from a background of personal experiences and ways of thinking that may not appear on the surface of the text, but may be of importance for the proceedings. It is also important to note that the language embedded in the culture is influenced by the respective roles and goals of the parties. In order to pursue their objectives, individuals use various strategies that are manifested as actions. Action as part of behaviour is, then, primarily linguistic.

In legal settings, interpreted speech is always communication-oriented; it should reach everyone equally. This is to ensure that both the authority receives the information needed to pursue its objective and that the parties using a language other than the *language of service* understand everything and are fully understood themselves. The primary goal of interpreting is to establish successful communication, which means that everyone involved in the communication should understand everything and be understood. Ideally, interpreters should always know what they are doing and why or when they say something. In reality, however, there are limits to what an interpreter can assure. There are situations when this is beyond the capacity of the interpreter to accomplish, for example if a litigant has not been sufficiently briefed by her legal counsel, or if there is no time to explain complex legal actions or concepts.

Language makes it possible to exercise legal rights and apply law. This is connected to the specific language of the courtroom, which is a reflection of the institution, which acts within a formal, standardised, predetermined and tradition-bound framework. The rituals, or dramaturgy, of the courtroom, such as putting on a robe or a wig, seating arrangements, the precise division of the proceedings into different stages and the clear assignment of who speaks when, are predetermined. Legal action is characterised by a precision of texts and discourses (incomprehensibility for laypersons notwithstanding) that nevertheless contain ambiguities in their wording. Legal professionals actively master both the meaning and the ambiguity of the texts and culture of the courtroom; laypersons are at the mercy of this language and culture.

Mastery of the language of the courtroom is directly related to professional and technical knowledge. It ranges from standard language to dialectal or colloquial expressions and idioms, but also to formal technical language in expert opinions or technical discussions. Professional and technical knowledge is understood here as the mastery of a specific field of expertise that is used by a person or group of persons in court proceedings and with which only this person or group is familiar.

This may range from the use of legal terminology to facts from other fields that are relevant in a court case, as well as the expectations of the respective setting and the cultural references that manifest themselves in the language other than the *language of service*. When it comes to interpreting in the legal systems, this acquisition of knowledge is primarily oriented towards the language and culture of the court. In interpreting, knowledge is directly related to understanding, because only what we understand can we express in another language, using the communication conventions of the target language. As a technical language, legal language forms its own register. Originating from general language, legal language is a closed system with its own fixed rules that only unfolds its meaning within the respective legal system and legal history of the country in question. Thus, in the context of interpreting, legal terms can only be understood within the respective legal system they belong to. This particularity of legal terminology must be considered especially in the case of polycentric languages (e.g. English in the USA versus the UK, French in France versus Canada or Senegal, Portuguese in Portugal versus Brazil or Angola, etc.).

In court interpreting, the 'foreign' is important in several respects. In addition to the languages used in the courtroom and the underlying culturally influenced behavioural patterns, the cultural specificity of the institution 'court' as well as the specialised cultures of certain subject areas also play an essential role. For interpreting in the courtroom, this may mean that the interpreter not only interprets from one language to another, but explicitates cultural references that are not generally known (e.g. in the language that is not the *language of service*) and facts that are not generally known (e.g. in the *language of service*) in order to achieve communicative success. To interpret language, as part of one culture, embedded in a particular setting that in turn is part of another culture, it is necessary to be familiar with both cultures and the norms and conventions of the respective setting. However, this knowledge alone is not sufficient: the culture-specific meaning, which is usually implicit in every source-language utterance, is not conveyed by the mere transfer of the linguistic meaning. The end user of the interpretation (the court or other parties to the proceedings) may lack the necessary background knowledge to understand it in full. Interpreters therefore need to make this meaning clear to the end user, e.g. in response to cues of non-understanding or misunderstanding, or even pre-emptively adding clarifications if the situational context requires. The knowledge is thus applied to two cultures – the culture of the foreign language and the culture of the court language – while also considering the subject-area knowledge. This is what characterises interpreting: the interpreters present the source information in such a way that it is also understood unambiguously and can be used as the basis for decisions by both the institution and the person being questioned – whether it is what to put forward next or a legal ruling.

3.3 Interpreting: norms and practices

Legal interpreting involves establishing communication between at least two languages and cultures in an interaction setting specified by the institution. This involves the transmission of spoken, written, signed or multimedia texts.

Both consecutive and simultaneous interpreting are used in *legal interpreting*. Simultaneous interpreting can be provided with the use of an interpreting booth or in the form of whispered interpreting (chuchotage), or as sign language interpreting. Simultaneous whispered interpreting allows the interpreter to convey information continuously about the course of the proceedings to the foreign-language party in an unobtrusive manner so that the proceedings can proceed without delay or disruption. It can, for example, be used when witnesses are being questioned, so that the accused can listen to the statements in real time and, if necessary, ask questions of the witnesses right away. Interpreters also resort to whispered interpreting when the foreign-language party cannot follow communication between lawyers or monologic components of a trial, such as opening statements. In court and public service interpreting, simultaneous interpreting booths are mostly only used in large court proceedings, particularly in the context of international courts. Small courts are rarely equipped with simultaneous interpreting facilities. Whispered interpreting, on the other hand, can be provided without additional equipment. Another form of simultaneous interpreting that is important in practice is *sight interpreting*. This is mainly used for technical court documents, such as statements of cases or indictments, as well as expert opinions or recorded statements.

The fundamental principles of interpreting can be summarised as follows:

- the rendition is in direct speech (exception: strategic use of indirect speech)
- the rendition is complete (translational completeness)
- the rendition is correctable or repairable (upon uncovering an interpreting error)
- the interpreter does not interrupt (especially during free narration, with the only exception being misunderstanding)
- the interpreter does not engage in side conversations (if this happens in exceptional cases, transparency is required)
- the interpreter takes notes (cognitive versus material memory)

The use of direct speech applies to both modes of interpreting:

Both in the simultaneous and the consecutive mode, interpreters speak from the *perspective of the speaker*.

The interpreter transmits the text as it was stated and uses the first person. However, there are situations where the interpreter takes on a reporting (outside) perspective and uses the third person. This makes it clearer who said what, for example when two people are speaking or there is overlap.

The change in perspective is often also used in chuchotage, where the interpreter interprets simultaneously whispering directly into the target language speaker's ear. The strategy here is also indirect speech: interpreting in the third person makes it clear to the end user when the speaker changes.

Whispered interpreting has the advantage that the parties perceive the verbal and non-verbal components of an utterance at the same time. It does not interrupt the flow of communication and saves time, which is important for courts and public authorities. In a criminal trial, the testimony of a witness who speaks the *language of service* can be whispered simultaneously for a defendant using a language other

Example:

Questioner: When did you leave the house?

Interpreter: Wann haben Sie das Haus verlassen?

Questionee: ***Ich*** *bin um 7 Uhr von zu Hause weggegangen.*

Interpreter: ***I*** *left home at 7 am.*

Figure 3.1 Direct speech in interpretation

Example:

Judge (to the defendant): Do you have anything to add?

Defence counsel: Your honour, you wanted to ask the witness for her address?

Interpreter (to the defendant, in the defendant's language): The judge asks if you have anything to add... Your counsel is speaking with the judge about the witness's address.

Figure 3.2 Indirect speech in interpretation

than the *language of service*. However, this mode does not allow the verification of the interpretation, since any other participants or audience at the trial who might speak both languages cannot usually hear the interpreter.

However, the dominant mode in court and public service interpreting is consecutive interpreting, which is typically used in dialogic settings. Consecutive interpreting refers to the interpreting mode in which the interpreter first listens to the source-language speech and then conveys it in the target language afterwards, i.e. consecutively. For the interpreter, this means that she has to store the source information in her memory for a short time, often using a special note-taking technique. This mode prolongs the duration of a hearing or *questioning*. Occasionally, the person presiding over the situation – e.g. the judge or *questioner* – will order the interpreter to provide a summary interpretation only, for example after a lengthy witness statement or after the counsel's statement. Summaries pose communicative, legal and ethical problems, as they can easily lead to a disadvantage for the foreign-language party to the proceedings. The European Court of Human Rights permits summary interpretation to a certain extent.

A full interpretation that is correct in both form and content is complete and conveys the spirit of what was said, without any additions or omissions.

When deciding on the scope of the interpretation, the fact that a full interpretation in the consecutive mode extends (usually doubles) the duration of the interview always plays a role. This can be avoided by making seating arrangements that allow whispered interpreting for the defendant, making it easier for the court or the authority to decide in favour of full interpretation.

If we consider interpreters as comprehensive transcultural communicators, they should be given more scope for action than is currently the case in judicial and administrative practice. The interpreters would then be holistic mediators of communication and culture who would not only provide the court or public authority with the rendition of the statement of an end user speaking a different language, but also with information that is indispensable for understanding. This flow of information would of course not be limited to this direction – the end user who does not speak the *language of service* is also entitled to comprehensive information and needs more in terms of translation and information than is currently the case. The decision on the extent of interpretation ultimately always lies with the court or public authority. Interpreters must know which topics and which material are relevant to the proceedings and the decision.

In proceedings in court and at public authorities, different types of texts are used in different stages of the proceedings. In legal settings there are oral texts, which are predominantly interpreted using bilateral consecutive interpreting, and written texts, which are predominantly interpreted using *sight interpreting*, but other ways in which interpreters might interact with them include identifying foreign official documents in the proceedings, or providing separate statements on texts or larger contexts, specific situations or behaviours. This part of translatorial action is cultural mediation. The communicators in this framework are, on the one hand, the representatives of the authority, who act as its agents, and, on the other, individuals or groups who appear in court primarily on their own behalf.

Analysing these text types from a generalised perspective can help us internalise how they work. This helps us choose the right interpreting strategy in a concrete interpreting situation. This is because the different phases of court or official proceedings fulfil different functions; and the actions that the different actors take in the course of the proceedings also have different functions and aims. It makes a difference to the interpreting strategy whether the defence lawyer is raising an objection, exercising her right to ask questions, discussing the further schedule of the hearing with the court or making a closing statement. At the end of an interview with the police or asylum authorities, the recorded minutes may be back-translated for the questionee before she signs them. This is often done through

Example:

Questioner: When did you see the defendant outside your house?

Interpreter: Wann haben Sie den Angeklagten vor Ihrem Haus gesehen?

Questionee: Ich glaube, es war am Mittwoch vor dem Einbruch ... nein, Donnerstag, am Donnerstag war es. So am Nachmittag ... vielleicht ...oder nein, es war schon finster.

Interpreter: I think it was the Wednesday before the break-in... no, Thursday, it was Thursday. Sometime in the afternoon... maybe... or no, it was already dark.

Figure 3.3 Preserved interpretation

sight interpreting. The way interpreters work and the mode of interpreting they choose is always linked to the concrete communicative situation. In court and at public authorities, the most appropriate mode of interpreting will usually emerge by itself. The interpreter then uses different strategies on a case-by-case basis, always with the goal of comprehension. It is also important to note that the function of a text can change: it may not always be identical in the source language and in the interpretation.

We distinguish between two basic ways, or types, of interpreting: preserved and customised interpreting.

In some *questioning* situations, it is important for the interpretation to be as close as possible in form and content to the original statement, i.e. preserved. As an example, consider a witness statement that involves the time of an event. Here, the exact wording is of great importance to how the statement is received and considered.

The same applies when the *questioning* focuses on the wording of a disputed contract clause. In such contexts, every word and every nuance of meaning have such significance that the interpretation should reflect the original with the greatest precision. The cultural and linguistic specifics of the original should be taken into account as far as possible while reproducing the contents of the source text using the grammatical and stylistic means of the target language. On the one hand, *preserved interpreting* should therefore preserve the grammatical structure, content, word order, parts of speech and style used in the original as directly as possible.

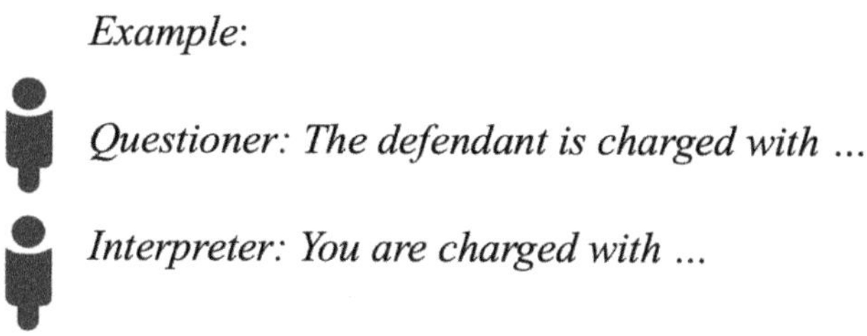

Figure. 3.4 Customised interpretation

Customised interpreting, on the other hand, aims to reproduce the original utterance in an adequate manner. The source text is the raw material for a comprehension-oriented communicative action adapted to the listener that is constructed in the target language. Customised interpreting is mainly used to make the arguments of the representatives of the authority comprehensible to the listener. This may involve changing technical terms into everyday language, and additions or explications may be useful and appropriate. Indirect speech may be replaced with direct speech.

As was explained above, certain persons do not have to testify in proceedings. Here, of course, the question arises whether it is legitimate for the interpreter to offer this additional explanation ('which means you do not have to testify'). From the perspective of comprehension-oriented interpreting, it is not a change to the text, but a *duplication* of information. The interpreter uses both the legal term used by the judge and the everyday language equivalent. The statements of the foreign-language parties and witnesses, however, should reach the court or authority unchanged, i.e. as preserved as possible, since they are usually essential to the proceedings. Any hidden (cultural) meanings that could be important for the court, however, can be provided as supplementary statements.

Regardless of whether preserved or *customised interpreting* is used, the original statement is always the source material. The interpreting process considers all aspects of the source material and attempts to render all relevant elements in a way that is appropriate to the purpose and situation. Factors of both text typology and functional pragmatics play a role here: depending on the text type and text function in the proceedings, the original utterances are reproduced as precisely as possible or adapted to the listener in the target language.

This guideline makes it easier for us to answer the question of how interpreters can provide an interpretation that is correct in both form and content in the very formal setting of courts and public authorities, where everything is done according to a precisely defined set of rules of procedure. We see that, especially in *questioning* situations, it is sometimes necessary to convey not only every single word, but also the finest nuances, such as stresses or pauses.

3.4 Action space and cooperation

Interpreters in judicial and administrative settings often find themselves in a situation where people mainly act on their own behalf, as laypersons who have no knowledge of the procedures of the authority or the court in question. The representatives of the authority, on the other hand, are familiar with every single step of the procedure. This can cause an imbalance between the communicators. Whether this disparity can be mitigated and the respective information presented in the interpretation to the respective foreign language speakers in such a way that they understand it fully depends on whether and how much room for manoeuvre the interpreter is given or the interpreter claims for herself in order to be able to carry out her task successfully.

Interpreting is an action. Translatorial action strives to coordinate its own concepts of action with those of others in a multipartial manner. This refers exclusively to allowing the participants in the communication to understand each other. This requires not only the mere reproduction of texts, but rather the ability to judge where participants, with their different roles, engage in actions that might be incomprehensible to others. The interpreter must then render these actions intelligible and functional for all participants in an appropriate manner.

The basic starting position that underlies translation, namely the inability of the communicating parties to establish communication themselves because of language and cultural barriers, is also present when it comes to interpreting *questioning*. Interaction in *questioning* situations involves situational factors that can be located at three levels: the institutional setting, the interaction constellation and the perceptual space. The communicators act in a certain constellation: the interview takes place in a predefined framework. The goals and the course of the interview are precisely predetermined, as is the distribution of tasks, competences or restrictions. Both individual and socio-cultural factors influence the text production of the participants. Extra-linguistic reality is thus incorporated into the text, into the language. The extent to which this happens depends on the precise distribution of roles in this complex system and the division of labour in it. The objectives of the individual participants within this system are defined depending on their respective role in a *questioning* situation and do not usually coincide with the objectives of the others.

Perception in a situation is closely linked to other areas of the human psyche, such as thinking, (previous) knowledge, attention, memory, emotions, etc., making perception an act of co-creation that involves the entire personality structure. We are thus prospectively involved in perception, and this involvement is influenced by structural features of our culture.

For people with different worldviews, patterns of behaviour and values, perception is based on their own conceptualisations and thought patterns, e.g. the way they perceive space and time. We know that time is experienced differently in different cultures. This, naturally, influences how we behave in time and space. As an example, consider punctuality, especially the expectation of the court that demands people be punctual to the minute. Members of different cultures may have a different perception of time, even for official occasions, and that may become evident in their (first) encounter with the institution. Visual and auditory communication signals also play a role in every act of communication, and speakers of other languages may not be familiar with them. They may also subconsciously interpret them through their own culture, which may change the meaning. Consider colour symbolism in different cultures or the different tempo of speech: speaking quickly or hesitantly, certain hand gestures or shaking one's head can have different meanings in different cultures.

Such moments are relevant for all actors, including the interpreters. In this context, the participants are simultaneously active speakers and active listeners who, on the one hand, consciously need to make use of the norms and conventions that apply, but who also subconsciously and automatically adhere to the conventions of their own country, culture of origin, language, etc.

Cooperation between interpreters and legal experts is essential for the success of *questioning*. The cooperation of the two professions in a *questioning* situation is influenced by various factors. This depends to a large extent on the interpreter's training and his ability to choose the appropriate course of action for a given situation. The choice of interpreting mode, for example, can have a significant influence on the dynamics of the interview.

Planning the *questioning*, briefing and debriefing together afterwards are essential aspects of cooperation. A lack of cooperation and preparation is reflected in the *questioning*. Questioning, as a form of institutional communication, is complex and places different psychological demands on all participants in such a communicative situation. The use of interpreters changes this dynamic and thus also the course and outcome of a *questioning* situation.

Finally, developments in the field of information and communication technology over the last two decades have also led to social and political changes. Communication at courts and authorities is supported by information and communication technologies, such as video conferencing technology, and these technologies are increasingly replacing onsite communication. This development creates lasting changes to communication and cooperation for all parties involved in legal proceedings.

3.5 Technology-assisted interpreting in legal settings

Various forms of communication and information technology can be used for interpreting in legal contexts. In large proceedings, where communication in several languages is required, simultaneous booths are used. This is mainly the case in international courts, e.g. the International Criminal Court, the International Criminal Tribunal for Rwanda or the Special Tribunal for Lebanon. Smaller (national) courts are rarely equipped with simultaneous interpreting booths; there, the simultaneous mode is often used in the form of chuchotage, or whispered interpreting. In addition to fixed booths, different mobile interpreting technologies can be used for simultaneous interpreting.

Whispered interpreting can be done with or without technical support. Technologies for chuchotage include portable interpreting systems and digital solutions, such as chuchotage via an app that is operated by the interpreter. The use of technology means that the number of people for whom chuchotage can be offered is not limited. It allows the interpreter to provide the interpretation via headphones for more than just two people without disturbing the communication in the room.

The use of video and audio technology – as extra-linguistic factors – can place different demands on interpreters and communicators in their practical implementation. Interpreting, as a special form of communication, is inevitably closely linked to the communicative behaviour of the communicators and adapts to it. Thus, if a judge decides to question someone via video link, interpreters will use interpreting strategies adapted to video technology for successful communication. The use of technology generally changes the communication conditions and may create completely new ones, depending on how the technology is being used. These external circumstances change not only the spatial distribution of the communicators, but also the communication and perception conditions of an interpreting situation. Thus, the use of video and audio technology creates new forms of communication because the technological support fundamentally changes the communication.

Perception is fundamental to every act of communication. The use of technology limits the available perception channels. In video interpreting, for example, perception is limited to two essential channels of information: visual and auditory. These limitations to perception are an essential part of technology-assisted communication. For interpreters and communicators alike, different technologies create different communicative requirements depending on the perception channels available.

For example, the quality of interpreting can suffer from poor technical conditions, such as poor sound or image quality or a lack of situational awareness of the interaction situation. In addition, difficulties are to be expected due to insufficient or lacking visual or auditory information, such as non-verbal communication cues, e.g. during turntaking or interaction. Since interpreting should consider communication as a whole on a multimodal level, the use of technology causes limitations. The multimodality of language includes linguistic, non-linguistic and extra-linguistic cues. In order to be able to reproduce what is said in the intended context, as well as to take into account the associated emotions, it is necessary not only to perceive the levels of multimodality, but also to transfer its meaning into the target information if needed, e.g. by verbalising a gesture that would otherwise not be understood.

For many parties involved in the proceedings, an audio or video link is the only way to participate in legal proceedings. In addition, logistical and security aspects should not be underestimated, for example when it comes to transporting inmates. In Europe, video technology has been increasingly used in the courtroom since the 2010s. Due to the ever-increasing need for interpretation, the reasons for the use of technology are generally similar across the world, such as saving financial, human and time resources.

A fundamental consideration in the use of technologies is that human and personal rights should not be violated. Even if the conditions of communication change with the use of technology, this must not influence the proceedings overall. The fairness of the proceedings must not be influenced or jeopardised by the use of technology. With the increased use of communication and information technologies, all participants in proceedings, including interpreters, will be confronted with their use and how this changes communication. In order for the conditions for a fair trial to be met, it is not only necessary to examine the appropriateness of the use of technology, but also to ensure that all participants in a trial are able to use and operate the technology used.

A lack of knowledge or insecurities in the use of the technology is a limitation in that it can affect the quality of the interpretation. In this context, internal and external factors that can cause issues should be mentioned as well.

Internal factors can cause stress for interpreters while working; these are connected to the individual interpreter and may be psychophysical or technical and operational in nature. Psychophysical factors include concentration difficulties, health impacts, strain on the vocal cords and psychological stress. Technical and operational factors include insecurity in the use of technology, insecurity about the subject matter to be interpreted and poor mastery of appropriate interpreting strategies and techniques. Since the onsite interpreting situation differs from remote interpreting, the strategies employed on site also differ from those used when technology is involved. Therefore, targeted strategies adapted to the technology must be employed. This often fails due to a lack of necessary awareness and formal training.

Various external factors can also cause stress. These include stress caused by faulty or inferior equipment and tools, noise pollution, inadequate lighting, physical discomfort due to poor ergonomics and distractions caused by other equipment. To prevent these disruptive factors, work equipment should be provided and prepared for use ahead of time.

Study activities

- *Modes of interpreting*
  - List the modes of interpreting you have observed in action or are proficient in.
  - Compare the key features of each mode of interpreting you have listed.
- *Cooperativity and translatorial action*
  - Describe a specific *questioning* setting, detailing all the actors involved. Discuss the scope of actions available to each actor.
  - In small groups, discuss the roles and expectations of each actor in the *questioning* setting. Identify which actors you found easier to describe and which were more challenging.
  - Share your findings within the small group and evaluate the effectiveness of the roles and expectations you have discussed for each actor.

- *Language variants*
  - List polycentric languages and their respective linguistic variants.
  - Is your language a polycentric language? If yes, list the variants you are aware of and the countries where they are spoken.
  - Create a terminological list of the ten most important terms from legal language in at least two language variants of a polycentric working language you use.
- *Technology in interpreting*
  - Describe the technology-supported forms of interpreting used in courts and government agencies in your country. Are different technological forms used?
    - If yes, analyse how the use of technology changes the dynamics of communication.
  - SWOT analysis on video-mediated interpreting in legal contexts
    In small groups, create a SWOT (strengths, weaknesses, opportunities and threats) analysis focusing on the use of video interpreting in legal contexts. This task can be done digitally or on a flip chart.
    - You can use digital tools or a flip chart for this. Divide the page into four sections: 'strengths', 'weaknesses', 'opportunities' and 'threats'. Illustrate each section with examples and fill it in for a comprehensive analysis.
    - Afterwards, compare your findings with another group's SWOT analysis to deepen understanding and gain varied insights.

Sources and further reading

Balogh, K. and Salaets, H. (2019) 'The Role of Non-Verbal Elements in Legal Interpreting a Study of a Cross-Border Interpreter-Mediated Videoconference Witness Hearing' in Tipton, R. and Desilla, L. (eds.) *The Routledge Handbook of Translation and Pragmatics*. London, New York: Routledge, pp. 394–429.

Berk-Seligson, S. (1990/2017) *The Bilingual Courtroom: Court Interpreters in the Judicial Process*. 2nd edn. Chicago, London: The University of Chicago Press.

Braun, S. (2017) 'What a Micro-Analytical Investigation of Additions and Expansions in Remote Interpreting Can Tell Us About Interpreters' Participation in a Shared Virtual Space' *Journal of Pragmatics*, 107, pp. 165–77 https://doi.org/10.1016/j.pragma.2016.09.011.

Braun, S. (2019) 'Technology and Interpreting' in O'Hagan, M. (ed.) *The Routledge Handbook of Translation and Technology*. Abingdon, Oxon, New York: Routledge, pp. 271–85.

González, R. D., Vásquez, V. F. and Mikkelson, H. (2012) *Fundamentals of Court Interpretation: Theory, Policy, and Practice*, 2nd edn. Durham, NC: Carolina Academic Press.

Hale, S. (1997) 'The Treatment of Register Variation in Court Interpreting' *The Translator*, 3(1), pp. 39–54 https://doi.org/10.1080/13556509.1997.10798987.

Hale, S. (2004) *The Discourse of Court Interpreting: Discourse Practices of the Law, the Witness, and the Interpreter*. Amsterdam: John Benjamins Publishing Company.
Havelka, I. (2020) 'Video-Mediated Remote Interpreting in Healthcare Analysis of an Austrian Pilot Project' *Babel*, 66(2), pp. 326–45 https://doi.org/10.1075/babel.00156.hav.
Kadrić, M. (2019) *Gerichts- und Behördendolmetschen: Prozessrechtliche und translatorische Perspektiven*. Wien: Facultas Verlags- und Buchhandels AG.
Licoppe, C. and Veyrier, C.-A. (2017) 'How to Show the Interpreter on Screen? The Normative Organization of Visual Ecologies in Multilingual Courtrooms with Video Links' *Journal of Pragmatics*, 107, pp. 147–64 https://doi.org/10.1016/j.pragma.2016.09.012.
Mikkelson, H. (2017) *An Introduction to Court Interpreting*, 2nd edn. Abingdon, Oxon, New York: Routledge.

4 Psychology of (interpreted) communication

Chapter summary

This chapter explains the psychological basics of *questioning*, starting with perception, processing and storing information. It highlights the interviewer's crucial role in influencing the interviewee's responses, introducing key psychological concepts like anchoring and framing effects. The text also integrates the context of interpreting, emphasising the significance of active listening, understanding and the utilisation of short-term and working memory in ensuring effective interpretation. It discusses the importance of thematic preparation for interpreting assignments and the transformation of information from the source language to the target language. The chapter further elaborates on the multifaceted nature of perception, memory and recall, underscoring the numerous elements and potential pitfalls that influence the reliability of statements within *questioning* scenarios. It accentuates the challenges in guaranteeing precise and dependable testimony in interviews and interpreting settings. Study activities in this chapter include transdisciplinary role plays and group discussions.

4.1 Perception and memory

In *questioning* situations, *questionees* are asked about events they have experienced, either because they were directly involved in the event (e.g. the accused and the victim in criminal proceedings, the plaintiff and the defendant in civil proceedings or the applicant in administrative proceedings), or because they perceived something about an event they were not directly involved in (witnesses). A person's internal thoughts and processes play only a minor part in interviews, such as *questioning* a defendant about her motive. The main subject of interviews are the perceptions of the person being questioned, i.e. events that she has seen, heard or

DOI: 10.4324/9781003301585-5

perceived in some other way. For the success of the interview and the assessment of the truth or falseness of a statement, it would be hard to overstate the importance of a statement being based on perceptions that were made, stored, retrieved and reproduced without error.

In practice, however, such statements are the exception rather than the rule. The process of perceiving a stimulus, mentally classifying and storing it, and retrieving it again in the context of an interview is subject to a multitude of possible sources of error, the existence of which people are generally little aware of. Confidence in one's own abilities, in the infallibility of perception and the accuracy of memory is widespread, both among people who are questioned and those who do the *questioning*. Studies show, for example, that the majority of people assume that the human brain records sensory impressions like a camera, allowing recordings to be reproduced in the mind at a later time. People also often assume that, once memories have been stored, they are no longer subject to any changes, just like a recording. However, this is not the case, as memories can change.

For interview situations, it is essential to be aware of these issues. Apart from situations in which interviewees deliberately do not tell the truth (see below), errors in the perception, storage and reproduction of experiences are by far the greatest obstacle to truthful testimony. In the following pages, we will describe some typical sources of error in these processes in more detail, although these limitations by no means occur in every case. Rather, a number of individual factors determine which sources of error become relevant to our perception, storage and reproduction of information in a situation. It is also not always possible to draw a clear distinction between these sections, so that some phenomena are addressed in several sections.

4.1.1 Perception

Perception, as the first part of the process that can later result in a statement, already contains a multitude of sources of error. Errors may arise from the stimulus itself or they can stem from the perceiver. We can distinguish between physiological factors and internal processes, which can both influence what and how we perceive. Many of the processes described below fulfil an essential function in our everyday lives. If we had to perceive and process all stimuli in our environment in the same way, it would be virtually impossible to navigate our environment in many situations. The ability to perceive selectively is therefore of crucial importance for coping with our daily lives, but it can be a disadvantage for the *questioning* context.

The first step is to realise that perceptions are usually sensory impressions. Accordingly, there must be a stimulus that can be registered by the human sensory organs. For this, the stimulus must have certain qualities. For example, the human auditory system is much less capable of hearing very high tones than, for example, that of dogs. In addition, the stimulus must exceed a certain threshold of intensity. The stronger a stimulus is, the higher the probability that it will be noticed. However, we need to consider that people can become habituated to stimuli – even quite strong ones – and no longer consciously perceive them. This is the case, for example, when people live near a train line. After living there for some time, they will no longer register the sounds of a passing train.

It is only when the stimuli to which one has become accustomed change that the probability that they are perceived consciously begins again. However, the contrast between the original and the altered stimulus is decisive. If the contrast is not sufficiently large and there is only a minimal, gradual change, perceptibility is barely influenced. Stimuli that are new to people have a good chance of being perceived. For example, if you drive the same route to work every day, it can easily happen that you do not consciously register some stretches of road because you are lost in thought. You see them, since you are driving in traffic, but you are not consciously aware of them. But if your usual route is suddenly interrupted by a roadblock, it is safe to assume that you will register it.

People have a rather limited capacity of consciously perceiving and processing several stimuli at once. Which of the many stimuli acting simultaneously on a person is actually registered depends, as described, on the quality of the stimulus (for example, a loud cry of fear will be perceived in almost every situation), but also on the person themselves. First and foremost, the capacities of the sensory organs play a decisive role. The eye, for example, is the strongest and usually the most important sensory organ for our perception. But it, too, has limitations. For example, we are not able to see or distinguish colours in the dark. A rapid change from a dark to a light environment or vice versa also limits the perceptibility of stimuli. These factors should be borne in mind when people make statements about situations that took place at night, for example. Another limitation is that the eye cannot perceive sequences of motion in detail if they exceed a certain speed. This can be important in connection with statements about a fight or an accident. In addition to these general capacity limitations, there are also individual factors, such as reduced visual acuity or limited hearing. In this context, it is also important to note that people who are being questioned do not always inform the interviewer of limitations of this kind, which can lead to them misjudging the reliability of the statement.

However, it is not only the capacities of the sensory organs that matter; the mental state in which someone is at the moment of perception can also have an effect on this. For example, strong emotional arousal, which can understandably occur when perceiving criminal behaviour, can limit our perception. A pronounced state of fatigue or alcoholisation also influence the level of detail with which people perceive their surroundings. Studies show that people who have consumed alcohol do not have more errors in their perception than sober people, but their perceptions are significantly less detailed. In general, the mood and emotional state someone is in can affect how she perceives the world around her. Consider a person who has just experienced a great success or, conversely, a person who has suffered a severe blow of fate. These two people might perceive and process the same situation very differently.

Besides aspects such as emotions, it is above all people's expectations that play a crucial role. Together with our interests, they control which aspects of the environment we consciously perceive and process. There are conscious aspects to this, in that people actively focus on certain things or events, which can lead to them blanking out and thus not perceiving other processes and stimuli around them. In addition, information that does not meet our expectations may also not be perceived consciously because we unconsciously filter it out. In contrast, people tend to fill in or interpret missing or contradictory content according to their expectations. For this purpose, *schemata* – patterns of thought – are activated that were created through earlier experiences and that have a connection to the current situation. If these *schemata* correspond to our expectations, there is a danger that we 'perceive' things that, in fact, primarily confirm our own ideas and expectations.

A well-known effect in this context is the so-called *halo effect* (Thorndike, 1920). It describes the phenomenon that people tend to infer characteristics of a person on the basis of one salient feature, although they have no actual knowledge of those other characteristics. For example, good-looking people are often considered to be more intelligent than people whose appearance does not correspond to common beauty standards. The *halo effect* plays a major role, especially when it comes to first impressions. People want to be able to assess their counterpart in order to adjust their own behaviour accordingly. If there is little other information available about the other person, we infer their entire personality on the basis of the visible features, including aspects such as clothing style and way of speaking.

4.1.2 Memory

When we consciously perceive a stimulus, it may be processed in such a way that we later remember the event. However, this is by no means always the case: countless things we perceive never pass from (ultra-)short-term memory into long-term memory. Our ability to recall them can be lost after only a few minutes. The second process that determines whether someone can give a statement on an event later is the transfer from *short-term* to *long-term* memory. But even if this happens and a memory is stored permanently, this does not mean that it is immutable and can be recalled at will. Stored memories are also subject to change. We will discuss both the way in which memories are stored and how they can change in this section.

After the first, perception-led phase of selection of which stimuli we even become aware of, there is a second selection process that determines whether a stimulus activates only the short-term memory or whether it is transferred to long-term memory. This is determined by various factors related to the stimulus as well as the individual. For one, the significance of the stimulus for the person perceiving it plays a major role. This is a mechanism similar to attentional control, which influences perception: if a stimulus or event is emotionally charged, personally significant or otherwise relevant to the interests of the person concerned, the likelihood of it being integrated into long-term memory is significantly greater than with incidental, everyday events. Another factor is whether it remains a one-time perception and there is no further examination of the stimulus, or whether the person affected reflects on it, perhaps discusses it with others or otherwise takes actions that mean that the event is replayed mentally and thus consolidated.

On the other hand, certain circumstances can contribute to making it very unlikely that a perceived stimulus is remembered, for example if the person experiences a strong physiological impairment immediately afterwards, such as a violent blow to the head or a concussion as a result of an accident. Emotionally upsetting events immediately before or after an event can also impair its retention – provided they do not already affect perception. In addition, retention can be affected by individual factors such as age – we generally remember things less well as we get older. Finally, different types of information have different probabilities of being remembered. In general, we remember information about people, especially people we have interacted with, or about objects that were relevant to the event better than, for example, background noises. But here, too, it depends on the situation and its significance for us.

Once a piece of information has been transferred to long-term memory, many people assume that it has been preserved for the future. But there are a number of mechanisms that contribute to human memories being subject to a constant process of change. On the one hand, very few memories remain as detailed over time as they were at the beginning; rather, details become hazy over time. At the same time, details can be added to memories that have nothing to do with the original event, or several different situations can merge into one event in our memory. There is an especially high risk of this happening when it comes to activities and processes that occur regularly in our lives – it becomes nearly impossible to distinguish one instance from another in retrospect.

Memories can also be altered through a defence mechanism, which can change our memory of events that do not conform to our self-image or worldview. Such a cognitive dissonance between our experiences and beliefs causes extreme discomfort, so people may reinterpret a situation using cognitive techniques to release the mental tension. This can cause us to suppress and deny memories that we experience as unpleasant. Another defence mechanism is rationalisation, where we retrospectively reinterpret events, for example by assigning ourselves an acceptable and morally justifiable motive for our actions.

Information that people receive about an event afterwards can also retroactively alter their memory of the event. This may be the case, for example, if there is media coverage of an event to which a person is questioned as a witness. If this person learns information from sources she considers trustworthy that does not correspond to her own memories of the event, her memory may be altered without her being aware of this. Of equal relevance in this context is the expectation of the interviewer, or communication of information that does not match the memory of the person being interviewed. If a person is not absolutely certain of his memory and is offered a plausible alternative by the interviewer, this can have a memory-altering effect.

These effects were demonstrated, for example, in a study by Loftus and others (1978), in which participants were shown images of a street scene that included a stop sign. In subsequent *questioning*, a stop sign was mentioned to one half of the participants, which was what they had actually seen, while a give way sign was mentioned to the other half. When later asked which traffic sign they had seen, a significantly larger proportion of those who had been told about a give way sign incorrectly remembered seeing such a sign. In contrast, among those who were told about a stop sign, the incidence of false memories was much lower.

This phenomenon can be understood within the framework of 'memory distortion', where the recollection of events is influenced by post-event information, leading to the creation of false memories.

Frequently, however, people are completely convinced of the correctness of their own perception and memory. Most people are not very good at assessing how reliable their memory is. Interestingly, this effect is particularly pronounced with regard to extraordinary events. Studies have shown that the quality and detail of memories of regular everyday experiences as well as of extraordinary experiences (for example, where someone was when they learned of the attack on the World Trade Centre on 11 September 2001) fade over time. However, people are much more convinced of the accuracy of their memories of extraordinary events than of everyday events. A person's assertion that they can remember an event in detail with certainty is therefore unfortunately not a reliable measure of whether that is actually the case. If, on the other hand, someone points out gaps and weaknesses in their memory, the interviewer should take this seriously.

4.1.3 Recall

Finally, different aspects of the situation in which a memory is retrieved and recounted are also important. In particular, the way the interviewer behaves plays an especially decisive role. It is her task to steer the conversation and to gain the information that is needed to continue working on the case. Accordingly, the interviewer usually has high expectations of the interview. These expectations may be perceived by the person being interviewed and can cause him to feel pressure to meet the expectations. In general, being questioned in court or by public authorities is an unusual and stressful situation for many people. Especially since the person being interviewed usually does not know which aspects of a statement make it useful for the interviewer, some people tend to answer as briefly and concisely as possible. This can lead to a very condensed recollection – much more so than would be the case, for example, in a relaxed conversation between acquaintances – and essential information may be lost.

At the same time, the interviewer may be subject to selective perception (see above) in the sense that she is more likely to take in information that is in line with her hypothesis and to ask for more details on that. She may be less receptive to information that does not support her hypothesis. Furthermore, the interviewee might notice this and, in striving to meet the interviewer's expectations, adapt his responses even more to the interviewer's assumptions.

Wanting to conform to expectations can also mean that the person being questioned does not want to deviate in his testimony from what other people have said.

For example, witnesses are often uncomfortable with having perceived something different or less than other witnesses. If the interviewer tells a witness that a piece of information she has given does not match that reported by other witnesses, this can lead to the interviewed person making a statement that agrees with the other witnesses due to her desire not to seem to have different views.

The way the interviewer phrases their questions is also of great importance. Various effects are known from psychological research that show that the wording of a question can strongly influence the response behaviour. One important effect in this context is the so-called anchoring effect, which describes the phenomenon that the human brain uses so-called *anchors* as reference points (Tversky and Kahneman, 1974) in decision-making situations in which the outcome of the decision is not absolutely clear. These anchors are information present in a person's mind at the decisive moment. This effect is particularly pronounced for numbers or estimates. It is important to note that the information used as an anchor does not necessarily have to be relevant to the question being answered. Experiments have shown, for example, that a number someone tells you and the result of a dice roll have an equally strong anchoring effect. This means that any anchors that the interviewer sets by giving information in the context of the conversation are very powerful and can influence the response behaviour of the interviewee significantly. The same, of course, goes for the way in which the interpreter words the interpretation. The interviewer might, for example, inform the interpreter during preparation of any intended anchors.

Similar dynamics can be observed in situations where the so-called *framing effect* comes into play. In this context, the interviewee's *schemata*, mentioned above, are of great importance. Through the wording of the question and the choice of framing, the interviewer activates corresponding *schemata* in the interviewee. The answer the interviewee gives is heavily influenced by these *schemata*. The phenomenon can be illustrated with the following example: when test subjects are asked whether they would undergo a very important surgical procedure, significantly more persons would be prepared to do so if the outcome is presented as a 75 per cent probability of a successful surgery and the condition being cured than if it is described as a 25 per cent risk of failure of the surgery with a subsequent deterioration of the condition.

4.2 Perception, memory and interpreting

Processes involved in interpreting, such as perception, memory and rendition in the target language, can be described as the acquisition, storage and retrieval of knowledge through the processing of information. This forms the foundation for organizing and rendering the target information.

It is acquired through the process of perceiving and absorbing information through active listening and understanding. We use our senses to perceive information, which is stored very briefly in ultra-short-term memory. Sensory memory contents disappear unless we pay attention to them. Through selective perception, we can filter out relevant information for further processing and transfer it to short-term memory.

It has already been established that a multitude of impressions and perceptions never make it from (ultra-)short-term memory to long-term memory. The crucial process for interpreting is the transfer of content from (ultra-)short-term memory to working memory. It is easier to remember new information if it can be linked to existing information or if the context is known. Therefore, activating prior knowledge not only aids in understanding but also in memorising information. For interpreting, this means that thematic preparation for the interpreting assignment is of utmost relevance.

From a functional-pragmatic perspective, interpreting is the transformation of information in the source language (source content) into information in the target language (target content). Source content includes not only linguistic input but also non-linguistic and extra-linguistic input. The images, concepts and terms created in the acquisition of source information are stored internally in the working memory.

In addition to memory, which can be described as a cognitive storage, interpreters use various memory aids, foremost among them a note-taking technique developed for interpreting. This interpreting-specific note-taking can be considered external storage: source information is captured in the form of words, symbols or numbers. During the rendition in the target language, the interpreter can retrieve them without significant cognitive effort and associatively link them with information stored in our working memory. Note-taking thus serves as a material extension of working memory. Key information, the structure of the source information and information requiring a great deal of processing capacity, such as numbers, names and dates, are particularly important to take down. Both what is taken down – whether in letters or symbols – and the arrangement of the notes on a notepad (analogue or digital) carry meaning and support memory.

Interpreting-specific note-taking serves multiple functions; it is not only external storage of information but also helps, through the way the notes are arranged, to evoke connections and associations that support the comprehension process and thus facilitate processing and rendition.

In traditional consecutive interpreting, material memory aids serve as the metalinguistic (re)production and visualisation of the auditorily and visually perceived source information. The result is a documentation of the source information that serves the subsequent production of the target information. Additionally, important notes for coordinating and moderating activities can be recorded, such as marking speaker changes or any misunderstandings that require (later) clarification. The notation can also support back-translations or be useful for cross-referencing with written minutes. All of this is only possible when the linguistically noted units are available in the source language.

Although we are capable of accumulating an unlimited amount of information, only a limited amount of active knowledge and information is available for processing. The information utilised is that which is in an activated state, i.e., in

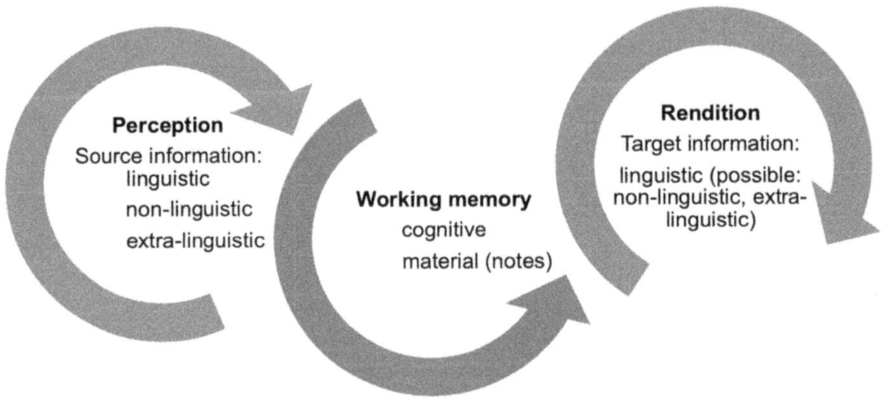

Figure 4.1 Translatorial processing

working memory. In interpreting – particularly in information gathering during *questioning* situations – the information should ideally be presented as it was in the source language – (in)coherent, flawed, (in)complete, etc. – both quantitatively and qualitatively.

Truth and falsehood play no role in the technical processing of information in interpreting. In practical terms the interpreter does not distinguish between them, they are interpreted alike.

4.3 Deception and lie detection

In addition to the various ways discussed above in which someone can misremember something and thus unintentionally give a statement that is not correct, there is of course the possibility of someone deliberately and intentionally making an untrue statement. One of the most important tasks of courts and authorities is to determine the veracity of the information received. It is therefore essential that the persons involved do so based on reliable and evidence-based criteria. In practice, however, people often rely exclusively on their own intuition. This is just as problematic as the long-prevalent practice of deciding whether a person is credible or untrustworthy as a whole. Extensive research in this area proves that this is by no means a personality trait. Rather, each individual statement must be examined for its credibility. But how can you tell if someone is telling the truth or lying?

4.3.1 Stereotypes and the ability to detect lies

When people are asked how you can tell if someone is lying, they usually mention certain characteristics that are considered to have a particularly strong indication effect. It is often assumed that certain non-verbal signals can be used to evaluate whether a statement is true or a lie. These assumptions are frequently based on the belief that people have less conscious control over their non-verbal behaviour and therefore the truth of a statement is more likely to 'shine through'.

For example, a large-scale study in 75 countries (The Global Deception Research Team, 2006) investigated what assumptions people have about how lies can be detected. They mostly mentioned non-verbal signals; only very occasionally were verbal or content-related aspects taken into account. The most common response was that liars avoid eye contact. Other frequently mentioned indicators included shifting their posture more than usual, touching and scratching themselves more often, telling longer stories than usual, making incoherent remarks, using gap fillers (such as 'um', 'uh', etc.), pausing while speaking and facial colour. However, as empirical research in this area shows, none of these features is a reliable indicator for determining a lie. Nevertheless, they are remarkably widespread stereotypes that people use to evaluate the behaviour of others.

These assumptions are not only common among lay people. Studies show that people who often have to determine the veracity of a statement in the course of their professional activities are also influenced by similar stereotypes. This applies to police officers and judges, for example, although of course it always depends on the individual and how he deals with this challenge. In this context, we speak of 'investigator bias', as studies have found that people working in such professions assume more frequently that a person is lying than laypersons do. However, this does not mean that they are fundamentally better trained to recognise untruths. Rather, the task that these persons have to perform due to their professional role is likely to make them generally more suspicious of statements than is the case with laypersons.

Humans generally do not have a very highly developed capability to detect lies. For example, a large-scale meta analysis showed that the overall share of lies correctly identified as such is around 54 per cent (Bond and DePaulo, 2006). This is barely more than basing the decision on a coin toss. It should be noted that many of the studies that were included in the meta study were based on experiments conducted under laboratory conditions, so their significance for the assessment of real statements is limited. Nevertheless, this low percentage is not surprising when you realise that people trying to detect lies often use criteria that are not very suitable for the task.

For example, various characteristics of the person being interviewed influence the likelihood that she will be believed, as do characteristics of the interviewer or how they relate to the interviewee. For example, people are more likely to be believed if their language, social background and other socio-demographic characteristics are similar to those of the interviewer. External features are also important; for example, attractiveness has a positive effect, as does a childlike facial shape and how a person is dressed is essential. Many of these characteristics are related to the halo effect described above in the context of perception, and they often influence our assessment of someone without us being aware of it.

Cultural factors must also be taken into account in this context. The strong focus on non-verbal behaviour requires that the person making the assessment be aware of its meaning. However, body posture, gestures and facial expressions cannot necessarily be interpreted the same way in every culture. Eye contact is a good example, as we have already seen that many people consider it important for determining whether a statement is true. However, eye contact – and lack thereof – does not signify the same thing in every culture. In Western cultures, it is considered polite and a sign of openness and honesty to look someone in the eye when speaking. In other cultures, however, this does not apply to every setting. Looking someone with a higher status than oneself – for example a judge – in the eye can be considered presumptuous and impolite. Here, a lowered gaze can be an expression of respect for the office and the person of the judge. However, if the judge is not aware of this, she might completely misinterpret the demeanour of the person being questioned. It is therefore the task of the interpreter, should he recognise the judge misinterpreting a gesture or other behaviour of the *questionee*, to alert the judge to this phenomenon in order to avoid a wrong assessment of the situation.

4.3.2 Lie detection markers: criteria-based content analysis – imposing cognitive load

So how can untruthful statements be recognised with sufficient reliability? In empirical studies, the examination of the content of the statement has proven to be significantly more reliable than the observation of non-verbal behaviour. Here, the technique of criteria-based content analysis (CBCA) is of great importance. It is based on the hypothesis that statements about situations that have actually been experienced differ in quality from statements that are not based on a real event (often referred to as the Undeutsch hypothesis after the German psychologist Udo Undeutsch, who established it). This is due to the fact that invented events are created from mental *schemata* based on typical sequences and storylines. In contrast, accounts of real experiences contain a number of characteristics related to content, contextualisation and the way they are told that are indications of them being based in someone's real life experience.

In a CBCA, a statement is analysed for the presence of these characteristics. Their presence is an indication that the underlying event is a real experience. The absence of these signs, however, is not a clear indication of it being a fabricated story, because there may be different reasons for their absence, such as an unwillingness of the interviewee to make comprehensive statements. Accordingly, even a carefully conducted CBCA can only provide an indication of the veracity of a statement. Inconsistencies in the presentation are conspicuous and therefore important for the evaluation of the statement. If, for example, long stretches of the statement contain many details and only a certain part of the statement lacks such details, this can be an indication that this part might not be based on a real experience.

The prerequisite for being able to carry out a CBCA at all is a comprehensive statement that is the result of a free narration by the person being interviewed. A short statement or answers to individual, concrete questions are not suitable as a basis for a CBCA, since most of the criteria do not occur in such a setting, even in experience-based statements. Accordingly, all parts of the statement must be long enough, because if the overall statement is extensive but the core event, which must form the basis of the legal assessment, is only described very briefly, a CBCA cannot be used either. The assessment is made on the basis of the analysis as a comprehensive evaluation of all the characteristics. It is not possible to determine a cut-off value that must be reached in order to assume that an event is experience-based. Rather, the presence and absence of all characteristics must be subjected to an overall assessment. The following is an overview of the most important criteria.

A basic requirement for an experience-based statement is that it is logically consistent. This means that there can be no irresolvable contradictions in the account and that it must also be fundamentally compatible with facts established from other sources. In terms of content, experience-based statements include significantly more details than fabricated experiences. They are anchored in a real environment in terms of time, place and sensory perceptions, which enriches them with information that most people do not or cannot invent for a fabricated statement.

Among the many details that can be recalled and recounted in a statement are various pieces of information whose presence also indicates a real experience. This includes, for example, descriptions of superfluous details, i.e. events that occurred around the same time as the core element of the statement, but which actually have no bearing on the case. It is precisely the description of unusual details that does not follow a schematic sequence of such a situation that points to a real experience. The situation is similar when it comes to recounting conversations or describing interactions between the persons involved. If it is a situation that was actually experienced, the sequence of these interactions follows an internal logic. If, on the other hand, the events are fabricated, there is no such logic, which often leads to a more schematic description. Disruptions and complications during the incident also tend to indicate that the account is based in reality, as liars tend to offer smooth and schematically consistent stories.

Because liars try to present themselves as trustworthy and competent and want to convince the interviewer of their account, it is unlikely for them to admit if the perceived event was not comprehensible to them. In reality-based narratives, however, this is more often the case. If a person describes an action or situation realistically, but without understanding its cause or meaning, this indicates an actual experience. This can be the case, for example, when a child reports sexual acts in a true-to-life manner, although the child cannot have any knowledge of them unless the child is actually a victim of them.

In experience-based accounts, the person recounting his own assessment and perception of his experience of the event also includes references to his own internal processes. Emotions, in particular, can leave a very strong impression in one's memory. A description of such emotions can therefore indicate a real experience – as long as it is not a stereotypical account of feelings that would be expected. This also applies to descriptions of perceived mental state and processes in other persons that they believe they observed. Here, too, a liar would have to fall back on schematic ideas that lack the individual aspect of describing a concrete observation.

The way an experience-based event is recounted also has special characteristics. Unlike fabricated stories, which are often told in rigid chronological order (also because the cognitive challenge of a different mode of presentation would be too great for most liars), real experiences are more often presented in an unstructured way. This does not affect the content, but the narrative often jumps back and forth, gaps may arise and be closed at a later time. The reason for this is that recalling memories, as described above, is not like watching a film, but is rather based on associations and interpretations.

There are also other characteristics of the presentation that point to an experience-based narrative. These include spontaneous self-corrections by the interviewee. These corrections or additions of details during the account come about because the ongoing recall process brings more details to the fore. However, self-corrections or slips of the tongue are not included in this criterion. Related characteristics are admitting gaps in memory and raising doubts about one's own statement. While a fabricated story is intended to convince the other person of the liar's point of view and is therefore usually presented as coherently and completely as possible, admitting that one cannot remember certain details tends to indicate a true statement. This is also because a liar has no interest in the other person making further enquiries – if the person says that she cannot remember certain things, the interviewer would have to obtain that information by other means. Liars tend to try to avoid this.

Experience-based statements also tend to reflect critically on one's own behaviour in the situation. If someone takes responsibility for what happened or argues in favour of the innocence of the person accused of the offence, these are also indications of a real event. This is also the case when responsibility is not attributed to the person, but to circumstances beyond the control of the perpetrator. Liars, on the other hand, have an interest in presenting themselves as innocent and in attributing the responsibility for the event to another person.

As we have mentioned several times, lying is a cognitive challenge that should not be underestimated. A liar not only has to fabricate a new story, but he also has to remember it immediately in order to be able to answer later questions correctly; he also has to monitor his own behaviour and the behaviour of the other person at the same time, as well as suppress the truth, which he knows. This involves a great deal of cognitive effort, more than simply giving an account of what actually happened does. The *questioner* can use this fact to her benefit: increasing the cognitive load can have a more pronounced effect on liars than on persons who make experience-based statements. This is referred to as the imposing cognitive load approach. One way to achieve this is to ask the interviewee to recount the described situation in reverse order. If it is an experience-based account, the person can use the internal logic of the event mentioned above. However, if someone has fabricated a story, he must first mentally restructure the narrative. The cognitive resources required for this can lead to cognitive overload, increasing the chances that the liar is less able intentionally to incorporate characteristics of experience-based narratives or that warning signs become more obvious. Another possibility is to have the interviewee draw the situation. Transposing a cognitively fabricated story into a graphic representation holds a great deal of error potential. Finally, asking unexpected questions can be very helpful.

Liars will generally prepare for their statement and consider what information the *questioner* might ask them. Asking questions outside the expected spectrum can throw the liar off.

4.3.3 Lie detection in interpreted interviews

What does it mean for lie detection when the interview whose content is to be analysed for truthfulness is an interpreted conversation? There is not much research on this to date, and the available results contain both indications that interpreting an interview could make it easier to detect lies and that it could make lie detection harder. More research in this area is therefore needed to gain robust knowledge on this important issue. In the following, we will look at the aspects on which there is already some research and that can provide initial indications on how to deal with interpreted interviews.

As explained above, to be able to assess the veracity of a statement using content analysis, an extensive, detailed statement is needed. However, many studies have shown that a statement contains significantly less detail if it has been interpreted. This could be due to people condensing their statements because interpreting takes time. At the same time, the interpretation may not contain all the details that were mentioned in the source language statement. Research shows that certain information is at particularly high risk of not being included in the interpretation.

Researchers have examined the frequency of three types of verbal cues in interpreted and not interpreted statements. They define complications as information that is irrelevant to the content of the statement but is nevertheless mentioned by the person being questioned. An example would be mentioning that they really like a dish that was served at an event but that is not the primary focus of the interview. This corresponds to superfluous or unusual information in the CBCA framework. Another cue is 'common knowledge details', that is, information about commonly known facts that lying persons incorporate into their statements to disguise their lack of detailed knowledge. This could be, for example, the description of a public place that the person being questioned knows, whether or not they were involved in the event that is the subject of the interview. Self-handicapping strategies, finally, are justifications that the interviewee includes in his statement in order to explain why he does not know something, such as having been distracted by something at a certain moment, which is why he cannot give specific details. Generally speaking, complications are an indication that the statement might be true, while common knowledge details and self-handicapping strategies are more common in false statements.

The question of whether this also applies to interpreted statements cannot currently be answered conclusively. However, there are certain indications that people include fewer complications in statements that will be interpreted than when they can communicate directly with the interviewer. The reason for this could again be that people might generally make shorter statements due to the necessary duration of the interpretation. There is also evidence of a different frequency of common knowledge details in interpreted statements and statements in interviews where no interpreter is present. Studies have shown that such details are less frequent in false statements when the conversation is interpreted. This may be due to the same temporal factor that also leads to fewer complications: due to this additional time during the interview, the interviewees have the opportunity to think of concrete details and have to fall back on general knowledge less often. The research regarding self-handicapping strategies is not clear. In some studies, there were no differences between interpreted and not interpreted conversations. In other studies, such elements were included in the source language statements, but it was found that they were less often conveyed by the interpreters. While this hardly reduced the content and meaning of the statement, it nevertheless means that the interviewers lacked essential information for assessing the credibility of the statement. It is therefore crucial that interpreters also interpret details that seem irrelevant. (To consider ethical issues that might arise from the interpreter's role, refer to the study activities in Chapter 2 and this chapter.)

Finally, very little is currently known about whether the techniques for increasing the cognitive load described above are still effective when it comes to interpreted interviews. However, initial results suggest that this is the case. One study, for example, showed that the request to draw the events in an interpreted interview also lead to the appearance of markers that indicate that the testimony might not be based on experience. There are similar indications for interviews where the witness is asked to recount their narrative in reverse order. However, as mentioned above, these are only initial findings; more research in this area is therefore needed to gain more robust knowledge in this area.

Study activities

- Exercise in *tandem*: Participants take turns telling each other about an experience they had in the past week. The other person tries to ask as specific and detailed questions as possible, covering all aspects of the experience (especially processes and sensory stimuli like what the other person saw, heard, tasted, smelled, etc.). The aim of the exercise is to reflect on one's own perception, on the one hand and, on the other hand, to challenge oneself to obtain such a concrete picture through *questioning* that an assessment of the situation is possible.
- Exercise in groups of three or four people: One person tells the group about an experience (e.g. from her last vacation, from an exam situation, etc.), and she can decide whether it is a real or made-up event. The listeners take notes and have to judge whether the story is true or fabricated. Before the reveal, the listeners discuss their perceptions and explain why they believe or disbelieve the story. Only then does the person who told the story reveal the truth.

Sources and further reading

Aamodt, M. G. and Custer, H. (2006) 'Who can best catch a liar? A meta-analysis of individual differences in detecting deception' *The Forensic Examiner*, 1, pp. 6–11.
Amado, B., Arce, R. and Fariña, F. (2015) 'Undeutsch hypothesis and Criteria Based Content Analysis: A meta-analytic review' *The European Journal of Psychology Applied to Legal Context*, 7, pp. 3–12.
Amado, B. G., Arce, R., Fariña, F. and Vilariño, M. (2016) 'Criteria-Based Content Analysis (CBCA) reality criteria in adults: A meta-analytic review' *International Journal of Clinical and Health Psychology*, 16(2), pp. 201–10 https://doi.org/10.1016/j.ijchp.2016.01.002
Anderson, R. C. and Pichert, J. W. (1978) 'Recall of previously unrecallable information following a shift in perspective' *Journal of Verbal Learning and Verbal Behavior*, 17(1), pp. 1–12 https://doi.org/10.1016/S0022-5371(78)90485-1
Bender, R., Häcker, R. and Schwarz, V. (2021) *Tatsachenfeststellung vor Gericht.* 5th edn. Munich: C.H.Beck.
Bond, C. F. and DePaulo, B. M. (2006) 'Accuracy of Deception Judgments' *Personality and Social Psychology Review*, 8, pp. 214–34.
DePaulo, B. M., Lindsay, J. J., Malone, B. E., Muhlenbruck, L., Charlton, K. and Cooper, H. (2003) 'Cues to Deception' *Psychological Bulletin,* 1, pp. 74–118.
Englich, B., Mussweiler, T. and Strack, F. (2006) 'Playing Dice with Criminal Sentences: The Influence of Irrelevant Anchors on Experts' Judicial Decision Making' *Personality and Social Psychology Bulletin*, 32(2), pp. 188–200 https://doi.org/10.1177/0146167205282152
Evans, J., Compo, N., Carol, R., Nichols-Lopez, K., Holness, H. and Furton, K. (2018) 'The impact of alcohol intoxication on witness suggestibility immediately and after a delay' *Applied Cognitive Psychology*, 33 https://doi.org/10.1002/acp.3502
Evans, M. and Meissner, B. (2013) 'Validating a new assessment method for deception detection: Introducing a Psychologically Based Credibility Assessment Tool' *Journal of Applied Research in Memory and Cognition*, 2, pp. 33.
Ewens, S., Vrij, A., Leal, S., Mann, S., Jo, E. and Fisher, R. P. (2016) 'The effect of interpreters on eliciting information, cues to deceit and rapport' *Legal and Criminological Psychology*, 21, pp. 286–304.
Ewens, S., Vrij, A., Mann, S. and Leal, S. (2016) 'Using the Reverse Order Technique with Non-Native Speakers or Through an Interpreter' *Applied Cognitive Psychology*, 30, pp. 242–49.
Falk, U. and Alles, M. (2014) 'Verhaltensökonomik und Anwaltsrhetorik: Ein interdisziplinärer Forschungsbericht zur Wahrnehmungsverzerrungen bei Risikoabwägungen, Prognosen und Richtigkeitswertungen' *Zeitschrift für Wirtschaftsrecht*, 35 (25/26), pp. 1209–18.
Hartwig, M. and Granhag, P. A. (2015) 'Exploring the nature and origin of beliefs about deception: Implicit and explicit knowledge among lay people and presumed experts' in Granhag, P. A., Vrij, A. and Verschuere, B. (eds.), *Detecting deception: Current challenges and cognitive approaches*, Chichester: Wiley Blackwell. pp. 125–53.
Kadrić, M. and Rennert, S. (2023) *Memorisierungsstrategien im Dolmetschprozess: Thesen, Techniken, Tools.* Wien: facultas.
Kahneman, D. (2011) *Thinking, fast and slow.* New York: Farrar, Straus and Giroux.
Lancaster, G. L. J., Vrij, A., Hope, L. and Waller, B. (2013) 'Sorting the liars from the truth tellers: The benefits of asking unanticipated questions on lie detection' *Applied Cognitive Psychology*, 27(1), pp. 107–14 https://doi.org/10.1002/acp.2879.
Leal, S., Vrij, A., Vernham, Z., Dalton, G., Jupe, L., Harvey, A. and Nahari, G. (2018) 'Cross-cultural verbal deception' *Legal and Criminological Psychology*, 23, pp. 192–213.
Leins, D., Fisher, R.P., Vrij, A., Leal, S. and Mann, S. (2011) 'Using sketch drawing to induce inconsistency in liars' *Legal and Criminological Psychology*, 16, pp. 253–65 https://doi.org/10.1348/135532510X501775.

Mann, S., Vrij, A. and Bull, R. (2004) 'Detecting True Lies: Police Officers' Ability to Detect Suspects' Lies' *Journal of Applied Psychology*, 89(1), pp. 137–49 https://doi.org/10.1037/0021-9010.89.1.137.

Meissner, C. A. and Kassin, S. M. (2002) '"He's guilty!"' Investigator bias in judgments of truth and deception' *Law and Human Behavior*, 26(5), pp. 469–80 https://doi.org/10.1023/A:1020278620751.

Niehaus, S. (2008) 'Merkmalsorientierte Inhaltsanalyse' in Volbert, R. and Steller, M. (eds.) *Handbuch der Rechtspsychologie*, Göttingen: Hogrefe pp. 311–21.

Reiss, K. and Vermeer, H. J. (2014) *Towards a General Theory of Translational Action: Skopos Theory Explained.* Hoboken: Taylor and Francis.

Simons, D. J. and Chabris, C. F. (2011) 'What People Believe about How Memory Works: A Representative Survey of the U.S. Population' *PLoS ONE*, 6(8): e22757 https://doi.org/10.1371/journal.pone.0022757.

Simons, D.J. and Levin, D.T. (1997) 'Change Blindness' *Trends in Cognitive Sciences*, Vol 1, Nr 7, pp. 261–67.

Steller, M. and Köhnken, G. (1989) 'Criteria-based statement analysis' in Raskin, D. C. (ed.) *Psychological methods in criminal investigation and evidence.* New York: Springer, pp. 217–45.

Strömwall, L. A., Granhag, P. A. and Hartwig, M. (2004) 'Practitioners' beliefs about deception' in Granhag, P.-A. and Strömwall, L. (eds.), The detection of deception in forensic contexts, pp. 229–250. Cambridge University Press https://doi.org/10.1017/CBO9780511490071.010.

Talarico, J. M. and Rubin, D. C. (2003) 'Confidence, not consistency, characterizes flashbulb memories' *Psychological Science*, Vol 14, Nr 5, pp. 455–61.

Taylor, P. J., Larner, S., Conchie, S. M. and van der Zee, S. (2015) 'Cross-Cultural Deception Detection' in Granhag, P. A., Vrij, A. and Verschuere, B. (eds.) *Detecting Deception–Current Challenges and Cognitive Approaches.* Chichester: Wiley Blackwell, pp. 175–202.

The Global Deception Research Team. (2006) 'A World of Lies' *Journal of Cross-Cultural Psychology*, 37(1), pp. 60–74 https://doi.org/10.1177/0022022105282295.

Undeutsch, U. (1982) 'Statement reality analysis' in Trankell A. (ed.), *Reconstructing the past: The role of psychologists in criminal trials.* Deventer: Kluwer 27.

Vrij, A. (2005) 'Criteria-Based Content Analysis: A Qualitative Review of the First 37 Studies' *Psychology, Public Policy, and Law*, 11(1), pp. 3–41 https://doi.org/10.1037/1076-8971.11.1.3.

Vrij, A. and Granhag, P. A. (2012) 'Eliciting cues to deception and truth: What matters are the questions asked' *Journal of Applied Research in Memory and Cognition*, 1(2), pp. 10–7 https://doi.org/10.1016/j.jarmac.2012.02.004.

Vrij, A. and Leal, S. (2020) 'Proportion of complications in interpreter-absent and interpreter-present interviews' *Psychiatry, Psychology and the Law*, 27, pp. 155–4.

Vrij, A. and Mann, S. (2006) 'Criteria-Based Content Analysis: An empirical test of its underlying processes' *Psychology, Crime & Law*, 12, pp. 337–49. 10.1080/10683160500129007.

Vrij, A., Fisher, R. and Blank, H. (2017) 'A cognitive approach to lie detection' *Legal and Criminological Psychology*, 22, pp. 1–22.

Vrij, A., Granhag, P. A., Mann, S. and Leal, S. (2011) 'Outsmarting the Liars: Toward a Cognitive Lie Detection Approach' *Current Directions in Psychological Science*, 1, pp. 28–32.

Vrij, A., Hope, L. and Fisher, R. P. (2014) 'Eliciting Reliable Information in Investigative Interviews' *Policy Insights from the Behavioral and Brain Sciences*, 1, pp. 129–36.

Vrij, A., Leal, S., Fisher, R. P., Mann, S., Dalton, G., Jo, E., Shaboltas, A., Khaleeva, M., Granskaya, J. and Houston, K. (2018) 'Sketching as a Technique to Eliciting Information and Cues to Deceit in Interpreter-Based Interviews' *Journal of Applied Research in Memory and Cognition*, 7, pp. 303–13.

Vrij, A., Leal, S., Fisher, R. P., Mann, S., Jo, E., Shaboltas, A., Khaleeva, M., Granskaya, J. and Houston, K. (2019) 'Eliciting information and cues to deceit through sketching in interpreter-based interviews' *Applied Cognitive Psychology*, 33, pp. 1197–211.

Vrij, A., Leal, S., Mann, S., Dalton, G., Jo, E., Shaboltas, A., Khaleeva, M., Granskaya, J. and Houston, K. (2017) 'Using the model statement to elicit information and cues to deceit in interpreter-based interviews' *Acta Psychologica*, 177, pp. 44–53.

Vrij, A., Leal, S., Mann, S., Warmelink, L., Granhag, P. A. and Fisher, R. P. (2010) 'Drawings as an innovative and successful lie detection tool' *Applied Cognitive Psychology*, 24, pp. 587–94 https://doi.org/10.1002/acp.1627.

Vrij, A., Mann, S. A., Fisher, R. P., Leal, S., Milne, R. and Bull, R. (2008) 'Increasing cognitive load to facilitate lie detection: the benefit of recalling an event in reverse order' *Law and Human Behaviour*, 32(3), pp. 253–65 https://doi.org/10.1007/s10979-007-9103-y.

5 Questioning and interpreting techniques

Chapter summary

This chapter looks at the general framework of *questioning* situations. It provides a comprehensive guide to the preparation and execution of *questioning* in various contexts, emphasising the critical role of thorough preparation to ensure the smooth progression of the interview. The text delves into the specifics of *questioning* different individuals, including children, traumatised persons and individuals with special needs, outlining the unique approaches and considerations for each group. It emphasises the importance of creating a comfortable atmosphere that encourages trust, ensuring the interviewee's understanding of the interpreting process and prioritising their need for information. Study activities in this chapter include group and individual work, interdisciplinary role plays and group discussions.

5.1 Structure of an interview

Like in other forms of social interaction, communication in a *questioning* situation takes place on multiple levels. On the factual level, there is an exchange of information, usually concerning facts and events. On the relationship level, however, the emotions of the persons involved matter. Disruptions at this level can have a lasting effect on the factual level and thus on the exchange of information. From the perspective of communication psychology, the *questioner* must not make the mistake of focusing solely on the factual level and ignoring the emotional aspects of communication, as this can cause the *questioning* objectives to fail. Unlike the factual level, it is not only what is said that is important for the relationship level, but also the overall behaviour, especially non-verbal communication such as body language, facial expressions, pitch or the proximity or distance between *questionee* and *questioner*. This aspect requires special attention and caution, as many of these non-verbal behaviours are strongly culture-dependent and have different meanings in different societies. Interpreting them according to the norms of one's own culture can therefore easily lead to misunderstandings.

DOI: 10.4324/9781003301585-6

The focus of *questioning* is to obtain information in order to establish the truth of the issues relevant to the case in question. This applies not only to criminal and administrative proceedings, but also to civil court proceedings. Although the parties generally have more leeway here with regard to the course of the proceedings than in criminal proceedings, the authorities or court must nevertheless always focus on establishing what actually happened when *questioning* someone. There can be a number of obstacles to establishing the truth, for example if the person being questioned is mistaken or is deliberately untruthful, as discussed in detail in the previous chapter.

Adding an interpreter changes the structure of the *questioning* profoundly. While *questioning* is usually conducted in a dyadic, or one-to-one, setting, the introduction of the interpreter changes this to a triadic structure, which creates new communicative constellations.

5.1.1 Preparation

Questioning situations present the *questioner* with a number of challenges. Not only must he always successfully convey that he is the one leading and directing the conversation but he must also extract as much information as possible from the *questioning*. He must have an overview of what *topics* should be discussed, what information is available and what can be shared with the person being questioned. Furthermore, he must observe the *behaviour* of the *questionee* and assess the *truthfulness* of her statements, as this is of great importance both for how to proceed during the *questioning* and with regard to the subsequent steps. Finally, he must ensure that the *questioning* can proceed smoothly and there are no disruptions. In order to meet all these requirements, it is therefore crucial to prepare the *questioning* situation comprehensively.

Involving the interpreter in the preparatory phase is an essential part of this. In advance of an interview, the *questioner* can inform the interpreter about the

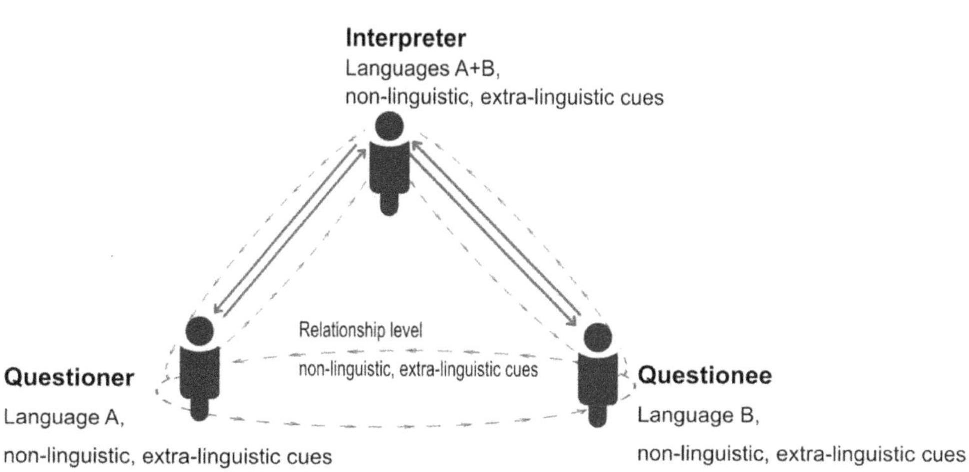

Figure 5.1 Interpreted interview situation

topics, expectations and participants in a pre-interview briefing. However, pre-interview briefings are not always possible, especially where time is of the essence.

The first step, in any case, is to decide who should conduct the *questioning*. There are many settings where this is clearly specified, such as in court, but in other constellations, there may be several individuals who could be considered. Attention should be paid both to how well the individuals know the case and to any special circumstances that might make it more likely for one person to obtain the information than another.

The interpreter can be given access to reference materials, court files, background information and transcripts or intercept records prior to the *questioning*. This facilitates a smooth interaction by allowing the interpreter to familiarise themselves with institutional settings and relevant context and terminology. (See previous chapter about working with both, written and oral inputs.)

Institutions can develop their own guides or formalised procedures to keep procedures transparent in an interpreted interview. This can help minimise potential problems and improve the quality of interpreting (Goodman-Delahunty and Howes, 2017). Formalised procedures are especially useful to provide structure when participants are connected via audio or video.

Finally, in certain situations it may be necessary to call in experts, e.g. an expert from the field of psychology for the *questioning* of a child or a potentially traumatised person, or technical and medical expert witnesses when it comes to a traffic accident that caused property damage and injured people, to name some of the most common cases.

Special demands are placed on interpreters when *questioning* a child or a traumatised person (see e.g. Salaets and Balogh, 2015; Amato and Mack, 2021). *Questioning* already poses a special challenge due to its objective.

Before the questioning, the interviewed child can be informed about possible interpreting modes and how interpreters work. During the *questioning* itself, it may also be necessary to prioritise the child's need for information. For example, it might be necessary to explain to the child clearly and transparently who the people present are (e.g. a psychologist or stenographer) and what they are doing.

Different approaches can be used when *questioning* children, such as adhering to the principles of non-suggestiveness and step-by-step structure (Salaets and Balogh, 2015, 47–50). The main objective of this method is to conduct the *questioning* in a way that does not suggest anything to the child. This requires special skills both on behalf of the police officer and the interpreter. The police officer must create an atmosphere of trust in which the child or minor feels comfortable telling them as much as possible.

Another special situation is interpreting for persons with special needs. This includes persons with physical, mental, sensory or psychological impairments who require individualised assistance and accommodations.

As we see, preparing for an interview also means the planning of the framework conditions. Insofar as the circumstances of the particular case permit it, the *questioning* should take place as soon as possible after the event concerned. The longer the time span, the greater the risk of the *questionee* misremembering something.

In order to schedule an interview with an interpreter as soon as possible, it may be necessary to use audio and video technology. The use of technology must be considered thoroughly with regard to the purpose of the interview as well as the parties involved.

It is important to ensure that the environment and spatial arrangement are suitable for a *questioning* situation. While in a courtroom, the seating arrangements are usually fixed, there may be more flexibility in, e.g., a police context.

The spatial positioning of the interpreter in relation to the *questioner* and *questionee* can significantly influence the dynamics of an interview. There are two possible scenarios for interpreters: with and without eye contact with the *questionee.* A common approach is a triangular arrangement, where the interpreter assumes a position that is equidistant from the *questioner* and *questionee.* This arrangement allows the interpreter to observe the facial expressions and gestures of both parties, which can be relevant to the interpreting performance. In addition, this position conveys *multipartiality*, as the interpreter is not seated closer to either one. If it proves to be favourable for the interpreting process or for the interpreter, then eye contact can be avoided where necessary.

Another arrangement that avoids eye contact and is especially used with sensitive topics involves positioning the interpreter next to the *questionee.* This approach aims to remove the interpreter from the direct line of sight of the *questionee* and thus direct their attention to the interviewer.

In audio- or video-mediated *questioning*, the interpreter may be remote, or on site with at least one party to the conversation, e.g. the *questioner* or *questionee*, while other persons are connected remotely. Eye contact is not possible in technology-assisted *questioning*: In audio-mediated interpreting no visual data is transmitted at all, and in video-mediated interpreting no eye contact can be established, which manifests itself in the 'eye-contact dilemma'.

As a rule, it is advisable to conduct interviews on the premises of the *questioning* institution (police, authorities, etc.), but under certain circumstances it may also be advantageous, if the law permits it, to question someone in a familiar environment, such as their own home. In certain situations, this can help ensure that the person being questioned is more relaxed and therefore more willing to provide information. Whether or not this is necessary or beneficial must be decided on a case-by-case basis.

In addition, the person scheduling interviews, if there are multiple in a day, must ensure that sufficient time is scheduled for each interview so that the next person does not have to wait, as long waiting times can have a negative effect on the mood and thus the willingness of the *questionee* to provide information.

This also means that when a *questioning* interview is interpreted (consecutively), the person scheduling it needs to be aware that interviews with consecutive interpreting take longer than monolingual or simultaneously interpreted interviews.

The order in which people are questioned must also be well thought out and planned. Finally, it must be ensured that the interview is not interrupted by people entering the room, the ringing of a telephone or anything else.

The documentation of an interview is of great importance for any legal proceedings, as it enables other participants to the proceedings to learn the content of the conversation on the one hand and has evidentiary value in the proceedings on the other. Appropriate precautions must therefore be taken to ensure that the interview is either recorded or notes are taken. In this case, it is preferable that the *questioner* should not take notes herself, so that she can concentrate fully on the conversation. Another person should therefore be called in to keep the minutes. The *questioner* also needs to prepare comprehensively for the interview. She must be familiar with the contents of the case file and the current status of the proceedings so that she can direct the situation accordingly and ask the right questions. From a legal point of view, preparing for *questioning* requires the *questioner* to gain a reliable overview of the legal issues and considerations that are of importance to the respective proceedings. This knowledge can be of great importance when conducting the interview and for selecting and wording the individual questions.

Furthermore, the *questioner* needs relevant information about the person to be questioned. This concerns not only the *questionee*'s personal data, but also things such as her social background, whether she has previously had dealings with the *questioning* institution and how she previously behaved when questioned. All this is crucial for the *questioner*'s planning.

It is advisable to record the relevant information about the *questionee* in writing, and to prepare a written guide for the interview based on the topics and questions of interest. This will ensure that no essential questions are forgotten and that the *questioner* always keeps track of what information can be shared with the *questionee* and when.

A debriefing between the interviewer and the interpreter allows them to address any challenges that occurred during the interpretation, such as distressing content. Being exposed to burdensome and in some cases traumatic content and experiences encompasses certain risks for both interpreters and other professionals involved. If the necessity of coping with this information occurs too often or the content of a testimony is too troublesome, the risk of so-called secondary trauma arises, involving symptoms such as emotional distress or hyperarousal. Therefore, monitoring one's own mental health and availing oneself of support if necessary is extremely important for people who are exposed to distressing content in exercising their profession.

5.2 Rapport building

Empirical studies (Collins et al., 2002; Vallano et al., 2011) show that the relationship between the *questioner* and the *questionee* is crucial for achieving the goal of obtaining as much reliable information as possible. A pleasant, non-threatening atmosphere makes it easier for the *questionee* to relax in a situation that is usually stressful. This has a positive effect on concentration and recall and can increase the willingness to share information. Therefore, the *questioner*'s task is actively to foster a positive relationship. In the literature, this short-term working relationship is called 'rapport', although the word is sometimes used to refer only to the initial phase of *questioning*, where rapport is established. Although this early phase is particularly important in terms of first impressions and starting the interview, which makes it especially impactful for the persons involved, it is important not to lose sight of the quality of the relationship over the course of the *questioning*.

The way in which the *questioner* builds a relationship with the *questionee* must always be tailored to the individual. There are no uniform procedures; instead, the *questioner* must consider the needs of each *questionee*.

If the *questioner* and *questionee* do not speak the same language, this poses a significant challenge for rapport building, as a shared language is an essential component of the rapport-building process. The presence of an additional person, the interpreter, adds another level of complexity to the interaction. The strategies used to build rapport in a dyadic constellation need to be adapted to a triadic constellation. This means that the rapport-building process is no longer direct, but fragmented and highly dependent on the interpreter. Since the relationship between the *questioner* and *questionee* depends on the relationships between *questioner* and interpreter as well as between interpreter and *questionee*, successful *translatorial rapport* building requires interpreters to recognise and implement the *questioner*'s rapport-building strategies.

The *questioner* should create an atmosphere in which the *questionee* feels safe and understood. As a first step, the *questioner* can introduce themselves and address the *questionee* by name. They can also start a conversation with neutral questions or topics that do not cause a stress reaction in the *questionee* before starting the actual *questioning*. This also gives the *questioner* the opportunity to observe the *questionee*'s flow and pace of speech, posture and syntax. This can prove useful if there are conspicuous changes to these patterns in the course of the interview, e.g. as a reaction to specific questions or topics.

The way the *questioner* approaches the situation and a friendly and open manner in conducting the *questioning* is of great importance for the rapport-building process. The *questioner* can signal interest in what the *questionee* has to say both through their posture and their facial expressions. This can be achieved by turning their body towards the *questionee* or mirroring their posture. Interest and attention can be signaled through various forms of active listening, such as nodding or brief encouraging comments.

Active listening is fundamental for any act of communication. In interpreting, it forms part of the interpreting process. Listening can be viewed as an internal process involving cognitive processes of comprehension and memory. However, it can also be seen as an external process that becomes visible through active listening behaviours that provide feedback to the speaker, such as nodding. This external process is particularly important when the interpreter is physically present in the same room and interacts directly with the interlocutors. The professional listening process (Viljanmaa, 2020) in interpreting takes place on a multimodal level, which means that eye contact and non-verbal cues such as lip movements are also taken into account while listening. The listening process can be affected by a wide range of variables that can support or restrict the listening process. These variables can include participants, the situation or the interaction between the participants. The factors influencing the listening process can be divided into internal and external filters.

Internal listening filters are individual and contextual requirements for listening, e.g. the role of the listener, their attitude or their positioning in a room. Internal listening filters include physical listening filters, psychological listening filters and listening filters shaped by the interpreter's experiences (Viljanmaa, 2020).

External listening filters include things related to the speaker, such as an unfamiliar dialect, or environmental elements such as disruptive noises or background noise (Viljanmaa, 2020).

It is important for the *questioner* to maintain constancy in his listening behaviour and not to show it only when the *questionee* says something that the *questioner* wants to hear. Otherwise, there is a danger of distortion of facts, as the *questionee* might elaborate extensively on the topics she received feedback on but not say anything about things to which she received uninterested or dismissive signals from the *questioner*. Everything said applies also to the interpreter.

It is important to prepare the *questionee* for the interview by explaining to them how the interview will proceed and what is expected of them, both in order to establish a relationship and for the general success of the interview. It is important to emphasise that the *questionee* should clearly state if she does not know the answer to a question or if she can tell the *questioner* has misunderstood an answer, e.g. because of an incorrect summary.

5.3 The questioning process

As a first step, the *questionee* is asked to recount their experiences or observations freely, with no interruptions or questions. This narrative should be the focus of the interview, as studies show that answers given to concrete questions in *questioning* contexts contain considerably more errors than a free narration. Ideally, the *questioner* should signal her interest through her body language and facial expressions, and only paraphrase what has been said to ensure she has understood it correctly. Any questions that arise during the free narration can be noted down for later.

For interpreters, this means a switch between monologic and dialogic communication, or text and discourse. In this model, the free narration would be considered a text, or monologic communication.

Interpreters need to know how texts and discourses are produced and received. Being aware of communication types or 'speaker types' (who is speaking to whom and for what purpose) makes it possible to classify these processes in interpreting by first determining the text or discourse function and then selecting the interpreting type and the corresponding strategies.

On the one hand, in monologic – or unidirectional – communication, a speaker speaks to (usually) several people from whom no immediate response is expected (although a monologue may be followed by a question and answer session as a dialogic element). Speeches, lectures and reports are typical examples of monologic communication. They are usually planned and structured in advance, whether they are presented freely or prepared in writing and read out. Dialogic communication, on the other hand, is bi- or multi-directional, i.e. two or more people take turns speaking. The individual utterances may be prepared or spontaneous, but even if discourses are perceived as spontaneous on the surface, they are usually planned and conducted with confidence, never losing the common thread. Even the informal parts of a formal discourse follow certain rules and procedures.

If monologic texts are interpreted consecutively, the text can be divided into several parts or interpreted all at once. Typically, this involves long consecutive interpreting, which requires appropriate memorisation. In dialogue interpreting, however, the length of the utterances can vary greatly, from a single word to several minutes. This type of discourse is particularly dynamic, as the interpreter participates in the communication as part of the conversational triad (or tetrad), and may also steer the communication to some extent. In addition to consecutive interpreting, chuchotage can be used in dialogue settings.

In the case of a free narration, however, it is advisable to interpret only after the interviewee has completed their monologue. The interpreter should not interrupt the *questionee*'s monologue unless absolutely necessary.

Following the free narration, the *questioner* will generally ask concrete questions to get the *questionee* to expand on the information. It should be noted that this part of *questioning* is more prone to errors than the free narration. This is due to various dynamics at play in interviews, such as the desire of *questionees* to be able to answer every question. This can cause them to invent things if they cannot remember or to create connections that do not exist. The *questioner*'s expectations can also influence the statement, in that the *questionee* wants to meet these expectations (often subconsciously) and adapts their statement to this effect. Even the wording of the question can influence this.

Generally speaking, the quality of the answer depends largely on the quality of the question–which is also connected to the quality of the interpretation.

An optimal question asks for a concrete piece of information and allows the *questionee* to give a clear, unambiguous answer. If two or more questions are asked at the same time, there is a risk that not all of them will be answered or that it is not clear which question an answer refers to.

Questions with complex sentence structures, double negatives, multiple connected questions, as well as colloquialisms, sociolects or hidden meanings can make interpreting (and communication in general) difficult and impact rapport building. The use of legal terms can also make comprehension more difficult.

According to the principle of cooperation (cf. Grice, 1975), the maxims of quantity, quality, relation and manner play a decisive role in direct communication.

Quantity is oriented on brief and clear text or discourse that focuses on the essentials and avoids verbosity–not only to save time, but also because it makes it more comprehensible. Suitable quantity means that the sentence structure is simple and concrete information is given. The sentences are therefore simply structured, contain concrete information and prefer everyday language.

Quality determines the comprehensibility using the parameters simplicity, structure and order, brevity and conciseness. While preparing for the interview, the *questioner* will consider carefully how to word their questions, what to focus on and what risks might be associated with a particular choice of words.

Relation distinguishes the important parts from the non-essential ones, the information is structured logically, and there is a clear throughline. This makes questions easy to understand. It also refers to the relationship level, such as the use of examples that are relatable to the *questionee* or stylistic devices such as rhetorical questions, analogies or figurative speech.

Manner refers to clarity of information. Language that is tailored to the other person and evokes associations or images is easier to understand. Manner is characterised by a number of parameters, with the unambiguity criteria among the most important: above all, questions must be clear for the *questionee*. In other words: short and quick to grasp, well-structured, clear and unmistakable.

Questions should therefore not be too complexly worded. The language the *questioner* uses should be tailored to the *questionee* and, following the principle of simplicity, either avoid technical terms altogether or explain them if that is not possible. The questions should not spark unwanted associations; neutral wording is essential. The question is instrumental in steering the direction of the answer, so words should be chosen with care. Provocative, reproachful or accusatory questions are rarely helpful because they increase the risk of incorrect answers–either because the *questionee*'s defence reflex is triggered or because the *questionee*, if she is convinced her answer is correct, insist on it and is no longer prepared to engage in conversation.

Verbal and non-verbal markers of rapport (Goodman-Delahunty et al., 2015; Dhami et al., 2017) can be used as additional stimuli in the interview. They can express solidarity, respect or sympathy. Addressing the *questionee* by their (first or last) name, using polite forms of address or asking questions to ensure the *questioner* has understood them correctly can be employed strategically, and the interpretation should of course reflect that.

As a very large part of communication takes place through non-verbal communication cues, the spatial positioning of the interpreter is crucial to allow visual contact. Non-verbal markers of rapport such as gaze can influence turn taking and, as a result, rapport building. Gaze direction can be used to signal attention and interest. Other non-verbal cues, such as intonation, posture and mirroring gestures can be perceived as supportive.

When interpreting rapport building, the interpreter should consider that what is being said can address the relationship or the factual level. At the factual level, verbal markers of rapport are used to verbalise agreement, while non-verbal markers of support address the relationship level. Interpreters need to recognise these markers and translate them into the target language where possible.

There is a wide range of verbal and non-verbal strategies and their effectiveness may vary depending on the specific *questioning* situation and the people involved.

Every speaker speaks their own individual language, which is characterised by a thematic and individual style and is distinctive. It may borrow from other languages, or sometimes even create words. The interpreter considers the individual characteristics of each speaker. Successful translatorial communication is built on two pillars that are fundamental to every interpretation: comprehensibility and target audience orientation.

Despite the individuality of expression, text and discourse types can be identified in communication, and knowing them contributes to successful interpreting. Target audience orientation is essential, as different people have different prior knowledge–this applies to both *questioner*s and *questionees*. It becomes visible at several levels, including the lexical level: technical language, for example, can be used and understood without context and it is unambiguous in its field–but only to those who know it. Understanding the situation, the participants, their communicative goals, prior knowledge and the power dynamics allow the interpreter to prepare strategies and choose the appropriate tactics in the interpreting situation.

Finally, especially when *questioning* people who have little experience dealing with such situations, it is crucial to emphasise to them that they should only answer a question if they believe they know the answer. If they do not, it is preferred to let the *questioner* know this and leave the question unanswered. Otherwise, *questionees* may tend to give an answer no matter whether they are sure because of their desire to meet the (perceived) expectations. The *questioner* can actively reduce this pressure and, ideally, eliminate it.

The *questioner* has different types of questions at their disposal for the interview. We distinguish open-ended and closed questions. Open-ended questions give the *questionee* a great deal of space to answer. They are generally preferable because there is a lower risk of influencing the *questionee*. Open questions often use words such as 'who', 'what', 'where', 'when', etc., such as 'What did you see when you entered the room' or 'What did you and the defendant talk about?' Closed questions, however, limit the possible answers, for example by presenting answers from which the *questionee* must choose (multiple choice questions, e.g. 'Was the car red, orange or brown?'), or by limiting the possible answers to 'yes' and 'no' (such as 'Did the defendant fire the gun?'). These questions have a far greater potential to influence the answer through (perhaps unconscious) suggestion. Studies with simulated interviews showed that open-ended questions that require a detailed narrative response are effective. Ratings of rapport after interviews with open-ended questions showed no differences between groups with and without interpretation, suggesting that the presence of an interpreter does not affect rapport building. Interpreters can support the spontaneous exchange of the speakers and thus help build rapport between the *questioner* and *questionee*.

In addition to these fundamental techniques, *questioners* have a number of *questioning* methods at their disposal, most of which were developed for use in police work. One such method, the effectiveness of which in enhancing recall has been proven in many empirical studies, is the cognitive interview. In addition to the free narration of events, the *questionee* is guided through four stages of mnemonics:

1. Context reinstatement
2. In-depth reporting
3. Describing the event in different orders
4. Describing the event from a different perspective.

These mnemonics, or retrieval rules, utilise different mechanisms of memory and recall to elicit more detailed and comprehensive information.

The first retrieval rule that is used is asking the *questionee* to mentally reinstate the context in which the event was perceived. The *questionee* is asked to picture both the external environment and revisit her mental state at the time. To help reinstate the environmental context, the *questioner* can ask questions related to the location, time of day or weather, ask the *questionee* to picture objects that were at the location, or ask her about smells or sounds. The *questioner* also asks questions related to the personal context of the *questionee*. The focus might be on the *questionee*'s emotional state at the time, what she was thinking about and what her spontaneous reactions were. All of this helps to trigger memories and associations that can shed light on new details.

These details are the focus of the second retrieval rule. The *questionee* is asked to report every detail, regardless of how important or unimportant it seems. The reason for this is that *questionees* sometimes consider details unimportant that might be relevant for the *questioning*. In addition, it also helps stimulate associations and improve recall. It is important to make it clear to the *questionee* that she should only report details she remembers, and not to add any details she is not sure about.

The third step is to ask the *questionee* to report the event in a different sequence than it occurred. This way the *questionee* does not simply repeat the information she has already given, but is forced to think about the event in a new way and report the memories she recalls.

Finally, the *questionee* is asked to describe the situation from the point of view of someone else. This may be a person who was involved in the event or another witness. This outside view can elicit new associations and bring details to the fore that had not been previously reported.

Another well-established interview technique developed by British police forces and comprehensively researched is the so-called PEACE-model. PEACE is an abbreviation for Planning and Preparation – Engage and Explain – Account – Closure – Evaluation. Each phase is characterised by special features that require specific actions on the part of the *questioner*.

In the first phase ('Planning and Preparation'), the *questioner* is required to prepare the interview comprehensively. This includes a complete review of the available material and the associated identification of the relevant topics and questions. The focus of the interview has to be determined and a plan drawn up on how to proceed during the *questioning*. The personal characteristics of the interviewee have to be taken into account and the practical arrangements for the interview made.

In the first phase of the meeting between *questioner* and *questionee* ('Engage and Explain'), the focus is on establishing a basis of trust. At the beginning, the reason for the interview is stated and the objectives are explained. The interviewee is asked to provide any information and details that he considers relevant.

This is followed by the phase known as 'Account', which is the centrepiece of the interview. The aim of this phase is both to obtain a comprehensive report from the *questionee* and to expand the information obtained by asking specific questions. During the *questionee*'s report, the interviewer uses his posture and gestures to signal that he is listening attentively. The interviewer can ask both open questions, which lead to a self-formulated description by the *questionee*, and closed questions, which are aimed at a very specific answer.

In order to avoid an abrupt ending of the interview, the *questioner* uses the following phase ('Closure') to summarise the content of the interview, giving the *questionee* the opportunity to add further information or to clarify any misunderstandings. Finally, the *questioner* informs the *questionee* of the ensuing steps.

The last phase of the PEACE-model ('Evaluation') gives the *questioner* the possibility to reflect on the content of the interview as well as the impressions gained from the *questionee*. The newly acquired information is compared with the information that is already known in order to derive further steps in the investigation.

Study activities

Questioning techniques in interviews

- Exercise example: The stolen wallet
  - In this exercise, four different types of questions are used: closed questions, open questions, leading questions and rhetorical questions. The exercise is conducted as a role-play between an investigator, an interpreter and a suspect.
    - Closed question: 'Were you in the park on the evening of 5 May?'
    - Open question: 'Can you describe your activities on the evening of 5 May in detail?'
    - Leading question: 'So you had no reason to be near the crime scene, did you?'
    - Rhetorical question: 'Who would be in the park at this time if they had nothing to hide?'
  - Suspect:
    - Closed question: 'Do I have to answer these questions?'
    - Open question: 'What happens if I choose not to answer?'
    - Leading question: 'You think I have something to do with the stolen wallet, don't you?'
    - Rhetorical question: 'Why would I steal a wallet?'
  - Instructions:
    - Participants should take turns playing the roles of the investigator, interpreter and the suspect.
    - Everyone should try to use the different types of questions in the exercise.
    - After the role-play, a discussion should be held about the effectiveness of the different types of questions in the interrogation situation.

- Interpreting role-play:
  - Find a news report that describes a current event. To find a report on an investigation, visit the EUROPOL (https://www.europol.europa.eu/) or INTERPOL (https://www.interpol.int/) websites.
  - Based on the report, create a set of questions you would ask a suspect or a potential witness.
  - Role-play: Form an exercise group with at least three people, each taking on a role: interpreter, *questioner* and *questionee*. Simulate an interview.
  - Reflect after the role-play on which questions were less challenging and which were more challenging.

Movie recommendations:

- Complex role of court interpreters
  - Series *German House* on DisneyPlus (2023) (https://www.imdb.com/news/ni63807961/)
- Linguistic (meaningful) presence in court through interpretation
  - *Amistad* (1997) (https://www.imdb.com/video/vi2161771289/?ref_=ext_shr_lnk)
- Interpreting technique: Chuchotage
  - Stefan Zweig: *Farewell to Europe* (2016)

Sources and further reading

Amato, A. and Mack, G. (2021) 'The Best Interest of the Child in Interpreter-Mediated Interviews' *inTRAlinea* 23 http://www.intralinea.org/archive/article/2539 (accessed 8 June 2023).

Dhami, M.K., Goodman-Delahunty, J. and Desai, S. (2017) 'Development of an Information Sheet Providing Rapport Advice for Interpreters in Police Interviews' Police Practice and Research, 18(3), pp. 291–305 https://doi.org/10.1080/15614263.2017.1291580

Goodman-Delahunty, J. and Howes, L.M. (2017) 'High-Stakes Interviews and Rapport Development: Practitioners' Perceptions of Interpreter Impact' *Policing and Society*, 29(1), pp. 100–117 https://doi.org/10.1080/10439463.2017.1293051

Goodman-Delahunty, J., Hale, S., Dhami, M. and Martschuk, N. (2015) *Effects of Situational and Relational Variables on Interpreting in High Stakes Police Interviews*. United States Federal Bureau of Investigation.

Goodman-Delahunty, J., Martschuk, N., Hale, S.B. and Brandon, S.E. (2020) 'Interpreted Police Interviews: A Review of Contemporary Research' in Miller, M.K. and Bornstein, B.H. (eds.) *Advances in Psychology and Law*, Vol. 5. Cham: Springer International Publishing, pp. 83–136.

Grice, H. P. (1975) 'Logic and Conversation' in Cole, P. and Morgan, J.L. (eds.) *Syntax and Semantics*, Vol. 3. New York: Academic Press, pp. 41–58.

Heubrock, D. and Donzelmann, N. (2010) *Psychologie der Vernehmung: Empfehlungen zur Beschuldigten-, Zeugen- und Opferzeugen-Vernehmung*. Verlag für Polizeiwissenschaft, Lorei.

Houston, K.A., Russano, M.B. and Ricks, E.P. (2017) '"Any Friend of Yours Is a Friend of Mine": Investigating the Utilization of an Interpreter in an Investigative Interview' *Psychology, Crime & Law,* 23(5), pp. 413–26 https://doi.org/10.1080/1068316X.2017.1290091

Howes, L.M. (2020) 'Interpreted Investigative Interviews Under the PEACE Interview Model: Police Interviewers' Perceptions of Challenges and Suggested Solutions' *Police Practice and Research,* 21(4), pp. 333–50 https://doi.org/10.1080/15614263.2019.1617145

May, A., Holt, E., Al Saeed, N. and Ahmad Sani, N. (2020) 'Legal Talk: Socio-pragmatic Aspects of Legal Questioning: Police Interviews, Prosecutorial Discourse and Trial Discourse' in Coulthard, M., May, A. and Sousa-Silva, R. (eds.) *The Routledge Handbook of Forensic Linguistics*, 2nd edn. London, New York: Routledge, pp. 13–31.

'Resources for Professionals: ChiLLS–Children in Legal Language Settings: Hearing a Child with an Interpreter: Legal Foundations' (2023) Available at: https://site.unibo.it/interpretazione-minori-chills/en/deliverables/for-professionals (accessed 30 May 2023).

Rudvin, M. (2005) 'Power behind discourse and power in discourse in community interpreting: The effect of institutional power asymmetry on interpreter strategies' *Revista Canaria de Estudios Ingleses,* 51, pp. 159–79.

Salaets, H. and Balogh, K. (eds.) (2015) *Children and Justice: Overcoming Language Barriers: Cooperation in Interpreter-Mediated Questioning of Minors*. Cambridge: Intersentia.

Viljanmaa, A. (2020) *Professionelle Zuhörkompetenz und Zuhörfilter beim Dialogdolmetschen.* TRANSÜD. Arbeiten zur Theorie und Praxis des Übersetzens und Dolmetschens 112. Berlin: Frank & Timme.

6 Cultures of communication and interpreting with a focus on evidence gathering

Chapter summary

As a core element of establishing the truth, *questioning* in preliminary and criminal proceedings poses particular requirements for the cooperation between interpreters and legal professionals or investigators. Interpreters may offer contextual and cultural insights that impact outcomes, making interpreting a dynamic interplay between customising and preserving, influenced by institutional guidelines. Effective coordination and intervention are vital aspects of this process. Study activities in this chapter focus on interpreting strategies and their application.

6.1 Communication and interpreting cultures

In many legal settings, the objective is to establish the facts of a case and to find the truth. This applies in particular to court and administrative proceedings but also to private proceedings for the preservation of evidence, as in the case of structural damage to a building.

In interview situations with user of a language other than the *language of service*, people of different origins, languages and cultures, with different expertise and different objectives encounter each other within a complex system. On the one hand, we have representatives of the authorities: experts who are very familiar with the goals of the institution they represent, and whose task is to pursue them. The institution's goals and directives are determined by law, for example that justice be served and societal peace maintained. In the individual proceedings, the objective is to establish the truth: a court, for example, must establish the facts of the case so that it can come to a decision. In the pursuit of substantive truth, the institution is required to be impartial, objective and effective.

The evidentiary proceedings – the part of the court procedure in which the individual pieces of evidence are taken – serve to determine the truth and the facts of the case. The most important types of evidence are personal evidence (*questioning*),

DOI: 10.4324/9781003301585-7

documentary evidence, visual inspection and expert evidence. Personal evidence is the examination of the parties and witnesses, while material evidence includes documentary evidence, visual inspection and expert opinions, as well as findings from forensic analyses (of physical evidence, handwriting, etc.). The court assesses the results of the evidentiary proceedings and then makes its findings, deciding on the version of the facts that it considers to be true.

In communication across professional, linguistic and cultural boundaries, expertise and culture are key concepts. Thus, interpreting is based on the principle that linguistic transfer is always also a transfer of knowledge.

Translatorial cultural competence is understood as cultural knowledge in at least two languages and cultures. Cultural competence, both regarding the interpreter's own cultural heritage and the second culture, means consciously managing behaviour and relationships and the way this organises the discourse; this is not done automatically or 'naturally', but purposefully employed in communication. In addition to the cultural component, which manifests itself in language, cultural competence also encompasses explicit knowledge about one's own and the second culture.

What do cultural aspects look like in the context of the courtroom? What realities do we encounter there? The interpreter's task is to facilitate communication between the persons involved in court proceedings. From the interpreter's perspective, there are two groups in the courtroom, whose language and culture are unknown to each other. For the purposes of interpreting, the representatives of the authorities and those speaking another language are groups who do not understand each other in terms of language and, at times, in terms of technical knowledge or culture. On the one side, we have the *language of service*, which is embedded in the national culture, and a (national) language and culture of the authority, often technical in nature, and on the other side, we have a language other than the *language of service* embedded in the respective culture of the speaker.

Professional (and individual) culture shapes language and language use. In the courtroom, for example, ritualised actions help to maintain a formal atmosphere. An example of this is rising when the judge enters or leaves the courtroom. This ritual conveys respect and symbolises the authority of the court, which is reinforced by the fact that it is compulsory.

In some contexts, the court staff explicitly order to stand up ('all rise' or 'be upstanding'), while in other cases it is taken for granted. For people who do not understand the court language or court culture, this ritual may not be immediately recognisable and feasible. Therefore, in such situations, it is up to the interpreter to make the ritual action and instructions explicit ('please rise') in the languge other then *language of service* to ensure that the person concerned is sufficiently informed and can react appropriately. The explicitation strategy ensures that the person who speaks a language other than the *language of service* is meaningfully (linguistically) present in the courtroom and can participate in the court proceedings in the same way as all other persons who understand the respective culture and the *language of service*.

It should be noted that the interpreter's scope for action varies in different legal spheres, as interpreters working in legal settings must strictly adhere to the instructions of the representatives of the courts and authorities and respect the way they conduct the proceedings. In the European context, the scope for action is relatively large due to the rights granted to persons who do not understand the *language of service* by the ECHR on the one hand, and the courts' often broad interpretation of the tasks of interpreters that at times considers them comprehensive experts, on the other. This sometimes grants interpreters the position of expert witnesses and thus creates room for comprehensive action. The role of the interpreter as an expert witness means that their skills go beyond language transfer. They may be called upon to explain complex linguistic nuances, bridge cultural differences and assist in the explicitation of technical terms. As a result, the interpreter is perceived not only as a language mediator, but also as a provider of expertise, which contributes to the effective and fair administration of justice.

This expertise must be kept strictly separate from any legal or other professional assessments; the interpreter is in no way authorised to do this (such as judging whether a statement in the language other than the *language of service* could be determined as a lie).

Interpreting is by its very nature a comprehension-oriented and multipartial transcultural activity. It is geared towards understanding, considering the compatibility of the plans of action, objectives and interests of all participants. The procedural knowledge required for this includes not only the mere reproduction of texts or discourses, but rather the ability to judge where the behaviour of individual participants in their various roles is not comprehensible to the speakers of the other language, and to present this knowledge and meaning in a way that is appropriate and functional.

In natural communication (used here to refer to monolingual communication, or technical communication within a professional group), it is not always necessary to use the exact right word. The utterances must 'make sense' within the existing knowledge. Communicators cannot ascribe meaning to a 'meaningless' utterance if the concepts expressed do not match the communicators' prior knowledge. Logically our practices of action emerge from this knowledge and the thought structures: our actions are also determined by how we experience reality and think about it. The 'same' reality is experienced differently by different people, and it is also interpreted differently. Our experience of reality depends on which features of this reality are considered relevant in our culture, which are selected and find their way into our language – i.e., are lexicalised.

If the interviewer and the person being questioned do not come from the same culture (including professional culture) and do not speak the same language well enough for the interview, there are further challenges that must be considered: The perception and assessment of the person being interviewed by the interviewer, and the involvement of an interpreter to facilitate the interview and to support the perception and assessment.

Interpreters are sometimes cultural mediators in that they take into account subject-specific and culture-specific differences in the interpretation in order to avoid misunderstandings. Depending on the interpreter's role, they may have more or less room for action in this regard. How they fill this room for action depends on the legal framework – which is structured differently in different legal systems – and on the interpreters themselves, their qualifications and their understanding of their professional role. Interpreting studies, supported by empirical research, calls for interpreting activities at public authorities to go beyond mere language mediation. In order for the interpreted communication between the parties involved in the proceedings to become functioning communication, more is needed than the mere reproduction of the text or discourse in a target language.

Any knowledge – no matter how trivial – presupposes a certain amount of prior knowledge. In a communication situation where the communicating parties can be assumed to have the same knowledge, even unspoken thoughts can be comprehended functionally. In communication, various cues help us understand the messages of others and to convey our own messages. These cues can be linguistic, non-linguistic or extra-linguistic.

Since communication is shaped by culture (including technical and professional cultures), these cues may differ depending on the culture. Such differences must be taken into account in both *questioning* and interpreting.

6.2 Linguistic, non-linguistic and extra-linguistic elements

In the context of an interview, the interviewer needs to consider not only the linguistic elements, but also the non-linguistic and extra-linguistic cues in order to be able to adequately assess the information and veracity of what is being said. It is important to bear in mind that posture, body language and gestures are strongly influenced by culture. Especially when dealing with an end user who represents the state, such as a police officer or a judge, very different behavioural patterns may emerge. This can be due, among other things, to the attitudes and expectations people have towards state authorities as a result of past experiences. Gestures also do not have the same meaning in every culture. An example of this, as mentioned above, is that looking the other person in the eye is considered polite in some cultures but disrespectful and presumptuous in others.

Cultural characteristics are manifested in communication and have an impact at all communicative levels. Almost every conversation includes non-linguistic and extra-linguistic cues in addition to linguistic cues.

Linguistic cues are linguistic elements that we use to convey our messages. An example of this is the tongue click 'tsk', which is used in many cultures as an expression of negation or astonishment. In other regions, there are sibilants ('tss') that are used in a similar way. In Spain, however, a lengthened s-sound ('ss') can be used as an affirmative expression, which can be misunderstood by people from other cultures.

Non-linguistic cues are physical or visual signals that we send to complement or reinforce our messages. Examples include gestures, physical contact, personal space and silence. For example, shaking one's head is used as an expression of agreement and affirmation in some countries, such as Bulgaria, Greece or India, while in many other parts of the world, it is understood as a negation. Another example is the ring gesture, where a ring is formed with the index finger and the thumb. In many parts of Europe and North America, this gesture has a positive connotation, while in France and Southern Europe it is negative. Laughter can also serve as a non-linguistic cue and, in some cultures, functions not only as a sign of joy or mirth, but can also express shame or insecurity, depending on the situation.

Extra-linguistic cues are cultural or social communicative elements that can influence communication. They include aspects such as dress codes, for example the use of robes by judges or mandatory suit and tie for lawyers, interior design and hierarchies, and the different ways in which respect is expressed to others or to older people in particular. These elements are culturally shaped and may be interpreted differently by different people.

If the interviewer is not aware of the meaning of certain cues in the interviewee's culture, she may interpret the interviewee's behaviour incorrectly. This might cause a statement to be classified as less credible because the body language shown by the person being interviewed does not correspond to the interviewer's expectations of the body language of someone who is assumed to be telling the truth. Although non-verbal features actually say very little about the truthfulness of a statement, they are often given more weight. Studies indicate that at a very fundamental level, statements made by people in other languages are judged to be less credible. The interviewer needs to be aware of this dynamic in order not to be subject to a misconception that could have a negative impact on the person speaking another language.

The inclusion of an interpreter in the interview creates additional challenges for the interviewer in terms of shaping the conversation and evaluating its content. In some situations, the question of whether interpretation is necessary at all cannot be answered clearly, e.g. if the person being interviewed speaks the *language of service*, but only to a limited extent. An interview in a language other than the *language of service* (such as a *lingua franca* or the official *language of service*) could mean that details are not understood and that the potentially longer time needed by the interviewee to understand the question and formulate an answer could have a negative effect on how the veracity of the statement is evaluated. On the other hand, resources need to be used efficiently, and there may also be tactical considerations: if the person being interviewed mostly understands the questions, she may have time to prepare an answer during the interpretation. Non-verbal communication can accompany a verbal expression or function as an independent expression. Interpreters take non-verbal communication into account in their interpretation when it reflects a linguistic expression.

If an interpretation is needed only occasionally during the interview, *stand-by interpreting* is an option. Here, the interpreter only interprets when the person being questioned cannot adequately express themselves in the target language or if one of the participants (interviewee, interviewer or interpreter) intervenes and requests that something be interpreted.

These considerations need to be weighed against each other on a case by case basis. If there are doubts about the language skills of the person being questioned, the presence of an interpreter is required as a principle of justice and rule of law.

If an interpreter is included, this needs to be addressed in the planning of the interview. This includes instructing the interpreter on what the interview will be about and how it will be structured. In addition, it should be ensured that the interpreter has the necessary competence for the interview in question, e.g. if the person being interviewed uses a certain dialect, the interpreter must be able to communicate in this dialect. The interviewer should also inquire whether the interpreter and the interviewee know each other. This can often be the case with members of smaller language communities, and can be problematic. If possible, such a situation should be avoided.

For the interpreter, in turn, it is a matter of professional ethics to report any conflicts of interest or even if he knows the end user he has been asked to interpret for. In practice, if such a situation occurs (and was not detected in advance), the participants often decide together on the spot whether the interpreter can continue the assignment or not, e.g., in the case of small language communities where most people know each other and have the same interpreter.

In interpreted communication, it is crucial that the statement be rendered unaltered. In this context, any cues, but also omissions, expressions of doubt, jumping from one topic to another, 'defective' statements and ambiguities must be processed and reproduced by the interpreter in such a way that the interviewer can perceive and absorb the information present at all communicative levels. Particularly when statements are made in a language different from the *language of service*, the interpretation should facilitate the *questioner*'s ability to assess the credibility of the communicated content.

If the *questioner*, on the other hand, deliberately phrases their questions in an unclear or ambiguous manner (perhaps for tactical reasons), it is equally important for the interpreter to faithfully convey this lack of clarity or ambiguity. In such instances, the interpreter plays a crucial role in transmitting not only the words used but also the intentional vagueness embedded in the questions. This ensures that the interviewee receives an accurate representation of the original communication, allowing for a fair and transparent exchange despite any deliberate attempts to obscure the interrogative intent.

We have a kind of mental script that provides us with instructions on how we should act in certain situations in order to conform to professional, social and cultural standards. Typified knowledge of course also exists at the level of linguistic expression. This knowledge influences the way we produce linguistic utterances and how we understand the utterances of others. These so-called schemata also contain collective social and culture-specific knowledge that is activated in connection with certain text types, phrases, words, etc. We can only understand a language if we know which experiences and interpretations of reality are associated with the individual words and grammatical constructions. Schemata thus provide a social and culturally specific pattern of interpretation that helps us connect language and reality.

An utterance must always 'make sense' within the framework of existing knowledge. If the concept expressed does not match our prior knowledge, the utterance is 'meaningless'. In interpreting, it is sometimes necessary to make the meaning (the 'sense') of an utterance explicit. This may also mean that ambiguous or 'meaningless' utterances must make sense to the interpreter, who has to understand their intent and take this into account in rendering the target information. By transferring the 'meaninglessness' order ambiguity, the participants can react to it as they see fit – either to clarify something among themselves or ignore it.

Anything said during a statement in court or before a public authority is in principle part of the evidence on the basis of which the authority makes its findings and draws its legal conclusions. As was previously stated, for statements in a language other than the *language of service*, the interpreted output is considered the evidence. It needs to be emphasised that the source-language utterance does not go on the record, but rather the target rendition. That is why it is important that the authority receive the complete statements given by the parties and witnesses.

Interviews are usually very dynamic, concentrated, one-off events characterised by orality or direct persuasiveness, and they are often very spontaneous, even if they have been prepared. An accurate interpretation should ensure that the source information content is transferred unchanged into the target language. The dynamics and spontaneity of the discourse add considerable difficulties to the task of the interpreter. Certain interpreting strategies (e.g. modification, reduction) and tactics, which will be discussed later in this chapter, significantly support the interpreter's work and contribute to optimising (interpreted) communication.

6.3 Linguistic expression in questioning situations

Oral communication is fleeting and usually not repeatable. This is all the more true for interpreting. All interpreting is characterised by the fleeting nature of the text, which results in the typical time constraints and the inability to control and correct the interpretation.

Narrative styles are individual and depend on various factors, central among them a person's ability to put facts into words in such a way that they are comprehensible even to people without prior knowledge of the subject matter.

The communication of courts and authorities is fundamentally characterised by depersonalisation. This becomes very evident in the fact that linguistically, there is no acting person (agent); as a rule, the authority and its representatives do not refer to themselves as 'I'. The representatives of the authority are acting not on their own behalf, but as judge, public prosecutor, police officer, etc. on behalf and by order of the authority. The individual opinions and intentions of the representatives of the authority are generally irrelevant. This depersonalisation is expressed linguistically by using impersonal wording or the passive voice for the authority's actions, e.g. 'The prosecution charges the defendant with . . .', 'The court finds . . .', 'XY is sentenced to two years in prison', etc.

The language used ranges from formal, institutionalised technical language with set phrases to standard language. Formal language is usually used when written texts are read out loud. It is characterised by complex syntactic structures and technical terms that many may be unfamiliar with; the spoken texts retain the static nature of written language. Representatives of the authorities also frequently use acronyms or make abbreviated references to complex issues. The intention of this approach is not as such to be incomprehensible. Rather, this use of language represents the 'natural' form of communication between experts.

These texts and discourses that are only comprehensible to experts are used in various situations, such as the reading of indictments, motions in court, when a sentence is passed and pronounced, in the defence counsel's replies, final speech, etc. The argumentative and appellative content of these texts is part of a strategy and is addressed to the other participants involved in the decision, who are the only ones who understand this language.

This highly specific language reflects the institution, which acts within a formal, ritualised, predetermined and tradition-bound framework. The rituals in the courtroom, such as the judge's robe and the seating arrangement, the precise division of the different stages of the proceedings, and who gets to speak when in which stage, are predetermined. The intention of all these rules is to create precise and objective discourses, which may nevertheless contain ambiguous word choices. Representatives of the authorities are well-versed in both the meaning and the ambiguity of the texts and discourses, while laypersons are at the mercy of the (technical) language and culture of the authorities.

The mastery of a technical language of a domain is directly connected to technical and expert knowledge. Technical and expert knowledge in this context is the understanding of a specific subject area that is used by an end user or group of end users in an official procedure and with which only this end user/group is familiar. This ranges from the use of legal terminology to facts of a highly specific subject a case is concerned with as well as the expectations of the respective setting and the cultural references that are expressed in the other language.

In recent years, there have been improvements in official communication. Due to societal and legal developments (e.g. accessible communication and inclusion) and efforts at participation in democracy in individual countries, authorities are communicating in an increasingly professional and person-centred way. Successful communication and messages reach people more easily and have higher acceptance.

The wording, content and medium can be adapted for specific target groups, such as older people, young people, linguistic minorities, people with special needs, etc. This increases the quality of the service provided by the public authority while at the same time increasing its acceptance and use, e.g. the use of digital services or even making it more likely that the authority is called at all (e.g. by members of a community who usually handle matters among themselves).

In direct communication with laypersons, language use ranges from standard language to dialectal or colloquial expressions and idioms, but can also include formal technical language.

The language of the user who does not speak the *language of service* can range from standard language to dialect to a lexically limited language (such as a *lingua franca*), depending on the individual. It contains experiences and ways of thinking that do not necessarily appear on the surface of the text, but which can be relevant for the proceedings.

Human beings are shaped by enculturation into the respective (sub)culture and socialisation into the respective society in which we live and usually consider our own experiences as the standard, as what is 'normal', and we include much of what is 'natural' and 'normal' to us in our communication.

People who come into contact with authorities are usually laypersons when it comes to legal matters. The interpretation between them takes place against the background of an encounter between a layperson and a professional, where there is a lot of unfamiliarity. This unfamiliarity can be either one-sided or reciprocal. All actors, i.e. the representatives of the authorities and the parties to the proceedings, 'naturally' introduce elements into the proceedings that are unfamiliar to others (often without reflecting on them). In communication with authorities, the following 'foreign cultures' are confronted with each other: 'Foreign' language(s) embedded in their specific ('foreign') culture, and the *language of service*, embedded in its specific institutional and professional culture.

However, narrative styles also depend on the physical and mental state of the narrator in the situation and how they are telling the story (interrupting a thought or skipping something, for example, can lead to a defective utterance). The nervousness associated with appearing before the authorities also shapes the narrative style of many persons questioned. Overall, we see that interpreting at public authorities and in courts comes with some difficulties. Nevertheless, it is important that the statements reach the court or authority unchanged. Essentially, all statements are part of the material on the basis of which the court or authority makes its decisions.

The interaction format and interaction context determine how active the interpreters' participation in the communication is and how much space they are given. As a result of a study on dialogue interpreting in a diplomatic and political context, Kadrić and Zanocco (2018) identified two levels of interaction management at which the interpreters' active participation was visible: the informative and the expressive level. The informative level concerns the presentation of the content, i.e. what an end user says, while the expressive level refers to how that content is presented in terms of (technical) language, cultural and individual features. This classification also applies to judicial and official proceedings (cf. Kadrić, 2019) and enables the interpreter the better strategically to prepare for interpreting assignments as well as to apply appropriate strategies or tactics situationally.

The interpreter coordinates their interpreting strategies with the communicative strategies of the other participants to ensure that everyone is understood. This happens not only at the informative level – in terms of ensuring that the information (oral text) is reproduced in the other language – but also at the expressive. This requires the interpreter to identify when someone is behaving in a way that the other party likely will not understand due to cultural differences, so that they can either convey the information contained in that behaviour in a way that the other party will understand or point out the difference to avoid misunderstandings if that is necessary. This could mean conveying expressivity, e.g. emotions that are perceptible only to the interpreter and not to speakers of other languages, or representing the vividness of an idiomatic expression rather than just conveying its semantic meaning.

In sum: the practical understanding of possible strategies includes not only the mere reproduction of the texts but also the ability to judge where individual participants in the communication behave and act in their various roles in a way that is not comprehensible to the other party and to either convey the information to the other party in a suitable and functional manner or to make the difference transparent.

6.4 Interpreting approaches: preserved and customised interpreting

A typical form of discourse that is often interpreted in legal settings are narratives that are characterised by features of orality, such as fragmented presentation, self-corrections, defective syntax and a predominance of the expressive level.

As an example, let us look at a defendant who is accused of damaging property, in this case the entrance door of an emergency shelter. He is asked to tell in his own words what happened that night.

> Questionee: The whole thing definitely happened before 10pm . . . I know they said it was after 10 pm, but that's not true. They told me I was late. But I'm never late, that wouldn't make any sense. Um, I've often spent the night at the emergency shelter, I know very well that you have to get there by 10 o'clock because that's when they close and they don't make any exceptions . . . They don't make exceptions. I was definitely on time, um, what time, I don't know, at quarter to 10, or maybe just before 10, but definitely before 10. Over the intercom he tells me: too late. I say no, it's before ten, but he just says: too late, closed. Um so then I tried to open the door, but it didn't work. Maybe I kicked the door once in anger, but definitely only once. I can't imagine that anything got broken . . . The door is not new anyway. Someone is always kicking it. The worst thing is that I'm now banned from there because of nothing . . . Because of a mistake they made.

This is a statement where every utterance, including pauses, hesitations or self-corrections, can be significant. Therefore, it is important that the interpreter transmit the statement in full and unchanged in both content and form. Only in this way can the authority form their own image of the speaker, accurately assess their statement and evaluate its truthfulness. The statements of foreign-language parties and witnesses should reach the court or the authority unchanged, as they usually make up the substance of the case and are central to deception and lie detection.

Interpreting, with its overarching goal of successful communication, involves a number of subtasks for the interpreter. In the context of translatorial action in official and court proceedings, these tasks include conveying a bundle of linguistic information from the source culture into the target culture in a specific context-dependent situation, presented using the linguistic means of the target culture. Some legal systems grant interpreters more room for manoeuvre than others, acknowledging them as experts in understanding diverse forms of (culture-specific) behaviour, modes of action and thought processes. The interpreter may be called upon to elucidate aspects of language use, such as the intensity of a particular (e.g. swear) word, the cultural associations of expressions or the significance of specific dialects. In some situations the interpreter may need to proactively step in, particularly in cases of evident misunderstandings or when, based on their linguistic and translatorial expertise, they are convinced that the content has not been comprehended ('Your Honor, the interpreter believes the defendant may not fully understand that statement'). It is not within the interpreter's purview to determine whether the court reacts to such an intervention by clarifying.

Interpreting is a constant decision-making process in terms of when and how to interpret. The approach chosen depends strongly on the purpose of the interpretation: is the objective to enable smooth communication, e.g. to ensure that a defendant understands the caution they are given, or is it necessary to preserve every nuance and hesitation of the text because it is part of the evidence? These are two fundamental approaches to interpreting, which are part of the functional-pragmatic school of thought: preserved and customised interpreting.

As we have seen in previous chapters, interpreting in *questioning* situations – what one might call evidentiary interpreting – needs to be as close to the source text as possible so as to enable the interviewer to assess the reliability of a statement or to use specific *questioning* techniques (e.g. avoiding leading questions). This calls for *preserved interpreting*, which reproduces all mistakes, gaps, hesitations, repetitions, contradictions and self-corrections of the source text, and might go so far as to preserve the grammatical structure, word order or word type, as every nuance might be crucial. The preserved interpretation is as close to verbatim as possible in order to give the interviewer or the decision-making authority access to as much of the 'source material' as possible so that they might draw their own conclusions based on the evidence presented.

The previous example of a defendant accused of damaging the door of a shelter illustrates the importance of a precise preserved interpretation. In order to be able to determine whether the statement is true or false, the court must hear the statement in full and as close to the original in content and form as possible.

As we saw with regards to perception and memory, there are many potential sources of errors when it comes to recounting a perceived event. Recall is also influenced by how the interviewer asks the questions to elicit the information needed for the investigation. The wording of the questions has a strong impact on response behaviour. As we saw, our brains use anchor points as reference, particularly when it comes to numbers and estimates, such as the time in the above example.

Of course, a person being interviewed might not just misremember something but lie outright. In order to aid lie detection, it is important that the authority gain a comprehensive view of the source-language statement and how the person being questioned is presenting themselves.

Customised interpreting, in contrast, focuses on comprehension. It preserves the content but presents it in a way that ensures that the listener will understand it unambiguously with the knowledge she has. This means that the form may change: technical language might be explained or replaced by more general terms, long complex phrases might be split into several shorter sentences or summarised, culture-specific expressions might be explained and the meaning of non-linguistic or extra-linguistic information may be made explicit. Despite these adaptations to the listener, the content and meaning remain the same – it is only expressed in a way that the end user will understand clearly. A customised approach might be appropriate to ensure that the defendant understands the technically complex legal language or to prevent misunderstandings that might result from a gesture being misinterpreted by the interviewer or a word having specific connotations that he is unfamiliar with.

The question of whether customised or *preserved interpreting* is appropriate in a given situation is one that interpreters always need to examine, and the strategy may change from one speaker to another. However, national legislation determines the scope of action of interpreters, and the representatives of the authority might decide to expand or restrict it in a specific situation. This, too, can influence whether the source information is interpreted customised or preserved.

Depending on the situation, the legal system and the actors involved, the interpreter may be asked to or even expected to provide contextual information and explain culture-specific meanings to the authorities that they might otherwise not be aware of. This is not the same as the finding (identification and description of facts) or opinion (conclusion drawn from these facts) of an expert witness, but in some legal systems, the authority may consider the interpreter's comments as findings to draw their own conclusions.

Interpreting can essentially be seen as an interplay between two types of interpreting: preserved and customised interpreting. When to use which type depends very much on the persons involved in a concrete interview situation.

As in any discourse, there are also mutual (textual) dependencies between the participants in interview situations – independent of institutionalised structures – although the actions of the different actors have different objectives and take place in isolation. Each action is performed in a predefined temporal sequence and builds on the output of the previous actor.

From structuration theory (e.g. Giddens 1984) we know that there is a close dynamic relationship between action and structure. Action and structure together ensure that interactions succeed. Structure is provided by rules and

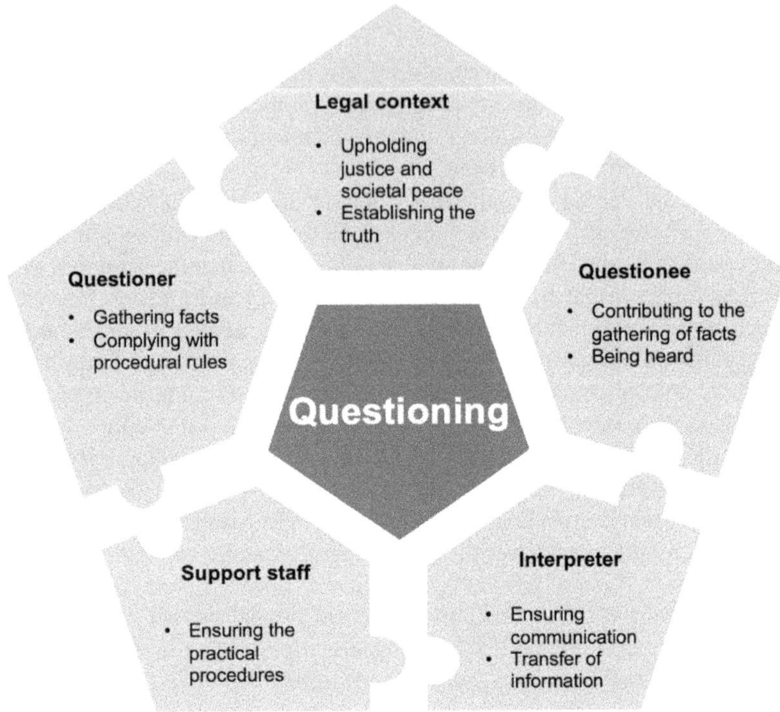

Figure 6.1 Questioning embedded in the larger context

resources, which the actors constantly fall back on. In relation to interviewing and interpreting, recurring (legal and criminological) themes and rules of an institutionalised framework, such as standardised or ritualised social practices, or voluntary commitments (professional ethics) can be considered core structural elements.

Every (inter)action includes coordinating and interventional activities of the individual actors.

The core objective of an interaction is to achieve a certain result. In this case, the desired result is the collection of a material that an authority needs for its further actions and decisions. Both the experts and the interviewees contribute to the collection of the material, usually with everyone being present simultaneously, either on site or remotely. This usually involves a certain method and the adherence to certain rules.

This form of interdependence requires constant exchange of information and mutual adaptation. The representative of the authority asks a question in the *language of service*, which the interpreter interprets into the language of the interviewee. Their answer is based on the interpretation and answers the question asked by the interpreter. The more precise and comprehensible the (interpreted) question, the higher the likelihood that the interviewee will give a clear answer and that the communication functions smoothly, ideally allowing the collection of material to proceed optimally. It also plays a role whether a third party is producing a written record of the interview.

The interview constellation shows clearly that the most important factors for successful collection of facts are communication and coordination between all participants. All participants must interact with each other, as they are all dependent on each other to successfully produce the 'product'. At the same time, it is important for all participants to be well informed about certain other factors. These include the subject matter, ideally also the time allocated for it, as well as the spatial and role-related positioning of the other actors. In Chapter 5, we discussed a guide to preparing and conducting *questioning* in various contexts, highlighting the crucial significance of thorough preparation for ensuring the interview's smooth progression. Good and structured preparation is also essential for the quality of the interpretation. Subject matter: Ideally, all those involved in the interaction are well informed about the topic. In this case, this includes not only the primary communicators, but also the interpreter and the clerk (the latter in particular if, for example, if the respective legal system permits a written record with summaries rather than it being a verbatim transcript).

(Spatial) positioning: In addition to the content, coordination is also required in terms of the exact spatial positioning of all participants, both formally – for example, through the seating arrangement – and in terms of content, for example ensuring that everyone can hear each other well or maintain eye contact.

The respective roles of the persons involved in the interview situation must be made transparent to the other.

Successful communication and interaction may not always be readily apparent, yet it hinges on the mutual dependability of individual actors. While all participants operate with a degree of autonomy within the confines of established rules and resources, which are continually (re)interpreted and reproduced, they also engage in ongoing reflection on their own actions and those of others. This reflective process prompts a continuous adaptation of their actions to the evolving context and analogous situations.

6.5 Interpreting strategies

Preserved and *customised interpreting* have different effects on the discourse: *customised interpreting* often improves the comprehensibility of a text, even to the extent of making the target information easier to understand than the source information. However, when *preserved interpreting* is required, interpreters will produce a target information that is as incomprehensible or redundant as the source information – even at the risk of being mistaken for bad interpreters. Studies in different countries and different legal systems show that interpreters switch between these types of interpreting as needed to ensure the success of transcultural communication, whether the goal is easy comprehension or exact reproduction

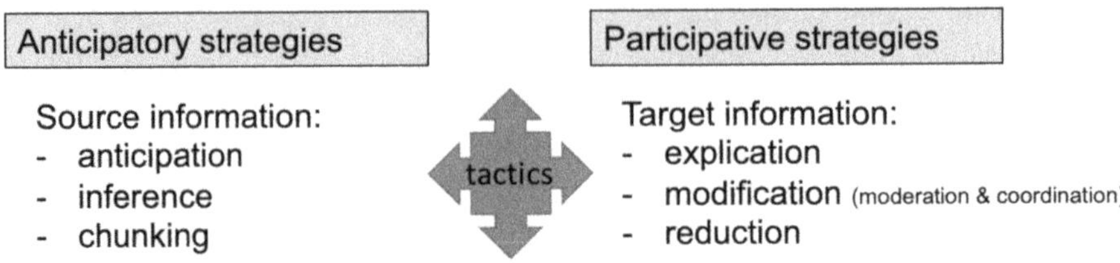

Figure 6.2 Strategic approach

The purpose of interpreting remains constant: the best possible conveyance of linguistic content to people who do not understand the original information. To achieve this goal, the chosen strategy can be tactically modified.

In the following, we will show how strategies are planned and what role tactics play in this process.

Interpreting strategies are an inherent part of interpreting competence. A *strategy* refers to the planning and preparation that is made in advance in order to carry out the interpreting assignment in the best possible way. This includes preparation of the topic and terminology, but also the analysis of the assignment and setting, which can allow the interpreter to determine which type of interpretation should be predominant. The interpreter may also be able to study the speaker in advance, e.g. to familiarise themselves with the persuasive and rhetorical devices he uses – for example in a court case with a defence attorney who is known for his sophisticated and unusual style of speaking. The interpreter could study the lawyer's public appearances to familiarise herself with the lawyer's speaking style so that she can anticipate it and participate better. *Anticipatory interpreting strategies* refer to the planning and preparation of an interpreting assignment in advance, considering the institutional and discursive framework. In the process of interpreting, anticipatory strategies entail the capacity to establish a level of predictability or foresee how information will unfold. This skill involves the ability to recognise patterns and try to foresee the progression of information while actively interpreting. *Participatory interpreting strategies* refer to the production of target information and involve specific interventions based on anticipation that the interpreter can use when the situation requires it.

The left side contains the major anticipatory strategies, which are established in preparing for the interpretation: Anticipation, inference and chunking. Anticipatory strategies are fundamental components of communication. In a bilateral conversation on a familiar topic, we can often guess how the other person will finish a sentence or thought, or infer what they said even if we did not hear everything. We also select and arrange information while listening.

The strategy of *anticipation* in interpreting means that we are able to predict how a sentence, such as a question, will end, based on the structure of the (technical) language and the topic. The more we know about the topic and the people involved, the more likely it is that we can also anticipate how the conversation will continue.

Questioner: Wie viele Personen haben Sie unmittelbar nach dem Zusammenstoß aus dem roten Auto steigen gesehen. (How many people did you see getting out of the red car immediately after the collision?)

An interpreter who is interpreting simultaneously (in a booth or as chuchotage) should be able to anticipate how the sentence will continue after 'Wie viele Personen haben Sie' ('How many people did you') based on their language skills, preparation for the assignment and the context. In a consecutive interpreting situation, the structural difference between German and English plays much less of a role.

A similar strategy is *inference*. Inference refers to the construction of meaning when we infer information that is not explicit from the thematic or situational context, or when we did not hear a word well but it is clear from the context what was said. The way (technical) language is used can give us clues or fill in gaps. Familiarity with the context and the subject allow us to draw logical conclusions and use the inference strategy.

Judge: You are . . . entitled to a lawyer

The first syllable in 'entitled' is not audible, but for the interpreter (and probably all participants who understand the *language of service*) the statement is nevertheless unambiguous: You are entitled to a lawyer.

The third important anticipatory strategy is the *chunking* of information. This refers to dividing information into individual segments, or chunks, so that their elements are unambiguously related to each other while supporting the organisation of the target text. Applied to note-taking, for example, it supports the interpretation process by the interpreter visualising the organisation of units of meaning and information, and presenting them in such a way that semantic links can be made and a coherent text emerges.

Anticipation is easier with highly formalised texts and discourses than with non-formalised texts on the same topic. Although technical texts are often very complex, their topic and type of text and discourse make them highly predictable, including structure, outline and terminology. The anticipatory strategies enable interpreters to reproduce the original text or discourse in a participatory way.

Participatory strategies include explicitation, modification and reduction.

The strategy of *explicitation* can be used for factual information, but also for subject- or culture-specific behaviour. Here, information that is implicit in the source language is made explicit in the interpretation. Nothing is added in terms of content that changes meaning, it simply provides unmistakable information, but the existing information is presented in a way that is comprehensible to the listener. Typical cases of explicitation in the official context are using the full form of an acronym, paraphrasing metaphors or proverbs, paraphrasing *realia* for which there is no direct equivalent, etc.

An interpreting tactic that is particularly suitable for situations with asymmetrical levels of knowledge is *duplication*, where, e.g., a technical term is given in technical language but then repeated in everyday language.

As with all strategies, the use of this, too, depends on the situation; if no explicitation is desired or appropriate, an incomprehensible term may have to remain just as incomprehensible in the target information.

Interpreters often make small *modifications*; for example, if the speaker corrects themselves, interpreters usually only interpret the corrected version. This does not apply to situations where *preserved interpreting* is required, such as a statement to the authorities; however, if the representative of the authority misspeaks or corrects themselves, the interpreter would generally take the *customised interpreting* approach and render the corrected version. Modifications are only made when the situation is completely clear and it is not necessary to ask.

Questioner: How did . . . when did you enter the country?

The context is clear, so the interpreter can interpret the corrected version: 'When did you enter the country?'

Modifications also include *moderation* and *coordination.*

If the interpreter asks a question to clarify whether something the speaker said was a mistake or if he did not understand something, or if the interpreter corrects their own mistake or points out that there has been a misunderstanding, this interrupts the interpretation. The interpreter changes their perspective and speaks as themselves rather than on the behalf of someone else. The interpreter might also take an active role in coordinating the discourse – for example, asking someone to speak into the microphone or telling a party who has understood the source language and wants to answer immediately that he still needs to interpret for someone else. We call this *coordination* and *moderation.* Moderation includes organising information in a way that everyone can understand. If, for example, several people have spoken before the interpreter had a chance to interpret, the interpreter can use gestures or mention the names of the speaker to make clear who said what. Switching to the third person to gain distance ('he calls you a . . .') or a change of function to a narrative 'they are insulting each other' also have a moderating function. Coordination, on the other hand, is more concerned with turn-taking and ensuring they can interpret, but there is some overlap with moderation.

Reduction a modifying strategy that concerns summaries or omits whole or partial units of information. Some facts that have to be expressed with many words in one language can be conveyed with one word in the other. Reduction is not a loss of information, but generally a compression of information. It may omit repetitions and redundancies that are not consciously used as a stylistic device, or utterances that are not necessary in the target information – for example, if the full name of something is used in the source text but it is better known by its acronym in the target language, the acronym suffices in the target text. In dynamic dialogues in which the participants interrupt each other or have little patience for the interpretation – especially if several participants speak the same language and therefore not all of them need the interpretation – interpreters sometimes summarise in order to not disturb the flow of the conversation or to keep up with frequent speaker changes. In this case, less relevant details may be lost, but the core content is conveyed nevertheless.

Interpreting strategies are supported by *tactics*. Tactics refer to individual decisions made during the interpreting process because the planned strategy has to be changed due to changed circumstances. Thorough preparation makes it possible to establish basic strategies – for example, what knowledge the parties can be expected to have and what might need explaining, or whether a particular person's manner of speaking might require a great deal of anticipation or chunking. In the interpreting situation itself, the interpreter can then react dynamically and use other tactics as needed – especially moderation and coordination are often used spontaneously.

The split-second application of interpreting strategies and tactics requires easily retrievable knowledge: Knowledge of the subject matter and the language, including grammar, semantics and pragmatics, i.e. its use in the context of the discourse.

Although interviews are usually one-time assignments for interpreters and the participants generally are different each time, they are characterised by a certain recursiveness: The interpreter is familiar with the range of likely topics in principle, they are usually told the subject of the specific case in advance (when they receive the assignment), the roles are predefined, spatial positioning is usually also predefined, and the time factor is usually also known. Knowledge of the overall situation allows the interpreter a broader scope of action and an effective application of strategy.

In official proceedings, the primary communicators come into the communicative situation with their respective different perspectives and expectations. Every action becomes the basis for further development, both for the institution and for those involved in the proceedings. Therefore, to guarantee fair proceedings, the aim is to ensure that all participants have the same opportunities for interaction in every procedure. As the description of the interpreting strategies shows, the interpreter can make a significant contribution to ensuring that transcultural communication is successful.

These findings correspond with research results from many countries, independently of the language pairs. Examples include studies by Berk-Seligson (1990/2017, 1988/2002) in the US, Morris (1995) on the well-known *Demjanjuk* trial in Israel, González et al. (2012) and Hale (2004) on Australian court proceedings, and Lee (2008), Ng (2009) or Cheung (2017) on interpreted court proceedings in Hong Kong.

However, we do not argue that the strategies mentioned above should be seen as absolutes. Such a position could be criticised in two regards: On the one hand, whether and to what extent the interpreter is allowed to use *customised interpreting* to provide additional information that the authority should have, and on the other hand, that even participants who speak the *language of service* do not understand much of it. The interpreter's comprehension-oriented approach would give foreign-language participants an advantage. The counterargument to this criticism is that in monolingual proceedings, the person conducting the proceedings is responsible for ensuring communication and can help ensure communication, but this ability to ensure communication is impeded by the linguistic and cultural barrier in proceedings with speakers of another language. The only person who can assess and recognise this in such a situation is the interpreter.

Study activities

- *Dimensions of communication*
  - Try to describe the linguistic, non-linguistic and extra-linguistic signals that are distinctive or prevalent within your language and cultural context?
    - Fill in the table and compare it with your colleagues

Communicative elements (intentional and unintentional)

Linguistic cues	Non-linguistic cues	Extralinguistic cues

- *Interpreting strategies*
  - Gain a deeper understanding of the concepts of 'preserved interpreting' and 'customised interpreting' by
    - Contrasting and defining them based on your readings from Nida (1964), and Venuti (2018). Drawing analogies: Create analogies to better understand these two types of interpreting. Use the following frameworks for your analogies:

      literal vs. free
      documentary vs. instrumental
      foreignising vs. domesticating

  - Identify scenarios: List real-world scenarios where each type of interpreting (preserved and customised) would be most appropriate.
  - Case study: Imagine you have an interpreting assignment. Develop a brief case study that outlines how you would approach a specific interpreting task. Would you choose a preserving or customised method? Justify your choice using your analogies and approaches from Nida (1964) and Venuti (2018).
    - Peer review: Exchange your case study with a classmate. Evaluate each other's work based on the effectiveness of the chosen interpreting method and the justification provided.

Sources and further reading

Auer, P. (1996) 'Context and Contextualization' in Verschueren, J., Östman, J.-O., Blommaert, J. and Bulcaen, C. (eds.) *Handbook of Pragmatics.* Amsterdam: John Benjamins Publishing Company, pp. 1–19.

Berk-Seligson, S. (1988/2002) 'The Impact of Politeness in Witness Testimony: The Influence of the Court Interpreter' *Multilingua*, 7(4), pp. 411–40. Available at: https://doi.org/10.1515/mult.1988.7.4.411

Berk-Seligson, S. (1990/2017) *The Bilingual Courtroom: Court Interpreters in the Judicial Process.* 2nd edn. Chicago, London: The University of Chicago Press.

Cheung, A.K.F. (2017) 'Non-Renditions in Court Interpreting' *Babel*, 63(2), pp. 174–99. Available at: https://doi.org/10.1075/babel.63.2.02che

Giddens, A. (1984) *The Constitution of Society. Outline of the Theory of Structuration.* Cambridge: PolityPress.

González, R.D., Vásquez, V.F. and Mikkelson, H. (2012) *Fundamentals of Court Interpretation: Theory, Policy, and Practice*, 2nd edn. University of Arizona Agnese Haury Institute for Interpretation series. Durham, NC: Carolina Academic Press.

Hale, S. (1999) 'Interpreters' Treatment of Discourse Markers in Courtroom Questions' *International Journal of Speech Language and the Law*, 6(1). Available at: https://doi.org/10.1558/sll.1999.6.1.57

Hale, S. (2004) *The Discourse of Court Interpreting: Discourse Practices of the Law, the Witness, and the Interpreter.* Amsterdam: John Benjamins Publishing Company.

Hale, S. (2014) 'Interpreting Culture. Dealing with Cross-Cultural Issues in Court Interpreting' *Perspectives*, 22(3), pp. 321–31. Available at: https://doi.org/10.1080/0907676X.2013.827226

Hale, S., Bond, N. and Sutton, J. (2011) 'Interpreting Accent in the Courtroom' *Target*, 23(1), pp. 48–61. Available at: https://doi.org/10.1075/target.23.1.03hal

International Organization for Standardization. (no date). 'Interpreting services: Legal interpreting: Requirements Services d'interprétation: Interprétation juridique et judiciaire — Exigences', ISO 20228 https://www.iso.org/standard/67327.html (accessed 27 September 2023).

Kadrić, M. (2019) Gerichts- und Behördendolmetschen: Prozessrechtliche und translatorische Perspektiven. Wien: Facultas Verlags- und Buchhandels AG.

Kadrić, M. and Rennert, S. (2023) *Memorisierungsstrategien Im Dolmetschprozess: Thesen, Techniken, Tools*, manual. Wien: facultas.

Kadrić, M., Rennert, S. and Schäffner, C. (2022) *Diplomatic and Political Interpreting Explained, Translation practices explained.* London, New York: Routledge.

Lee, J. (2008) 'Rating Scales for Interpreting Performance Assessment', *The Interpreter and Translator Trainer* 2(2), pp. 165–84. Available at: https://doi.org/10.1080/1750399X.2008.10798772

May, A., Holt, E., Al Saeed, N. and Ahmad Sani, N. (2020) 'Legal Talk: Socio-pragmatic Aspects of Legal Questioning: Police Interviews, Prosecutorial Discourse and Trial Discourse' in Coulthard, M., May, A. and Sousa-Silva, R. (eds.) *The Routledge Handbook of Forensic Linguistics,* 2nd edn. London, New York: Routledge, pp. 13–31.

Ng, E.N.S. (2009) '3. The Tension Between Adequacy and Acceptability in Legal Interpreting and Translation' in Feinauer, I., Marais, A. and Swart, M. (eds.) *Translation Flows,* Amsterdam: John Benjamins Publishing Company, pp. 37–54.

Nida, E. (1964) *Toward a Science of Translating: With Special Reference to Principles and Procedures Involved in Bible Translating.* Leiden: E. J. Brill.

Poyatos, F. (1993) *Paralanguage: A Linguistic and Interdisciplinary Approach to Interactive Speech and Sound.* Amsterdam, Philadelphia: John Benjamins Publishing Company.

Venuti, L. (2018) *The Translator's Invisibility: A History of Translation*, 3rd edn. London, New York: Routledge.

7 Hybridity of communication as a challenge for interpersonal communication

Chapter summary

This chapter discusses different hybrid forms of communication. Translatorial action requires specific transfer strategies when it involves rendering spoken language in writing (e.g. producing a wiretap transcript or forensic translation) or written language in speech (e.g. sight interpreting). As part of the translatorial responsibilities in legal settings, there is also a discrepancy between bidirectional and unidirectional language. Another form of hybridity is created through the use of technology. Distance interpreting (e.g. audio- and video-mediated interpreting) creates challenges not present in in-situ communication, where all participants are gathered in the same location. Distance interpreting combines different forms of interpreting modalities, e.g. with participants in one location and the interpreter working remotely, or participants at two or more sites. Depending on the interpreting modality, there are differences in the availability of visual and auditive cues, which requires an adaptation of interpreting strategies. Study activities in this chapter include interdisciplinary role plays and group discussions.

7.1 Understanding and interprofessional cooperation

The prerequisite for successful communication is *understanding*. Understanding, in turn, requires comprehending the content and grasping the context in which the subject matter is situated. These two elements, the comprehension of content and context, can in turn be subdivided into several components. The first step towards comprehension is to hear an utterance correctly in order then to process it. Comprehension happens on the basis of interpretations that build on existing knowledge and facilitate the comprehension process. Interpretations are mental representations in the brain that create meaning from sensory impressions and previous experiences. These interpretations are always influenced by our own linguistic, professional and cultural experiences, and world views. This means that the message we

DOI: 10.4324/9781003301585-8

receive is always an interpretation. This interpretation determines how we perceive its meaning and how we make sense of and evaluate other people's actions. The interpretation can always be something other than what was intended by the sender, so there is always a risk of a discrepancy between the information sent and the information received. This applies to communication in a shared language and to interpreted communication alike. Misunderstandings can occur, for example, due to different professional and world knowledge or linguistic ambiguities. However, interpretation considers not only the words, but also non-verbal and extra-verbal communication elements: eye contact and body language can reinforce a message or express understanding and empathy, especially in emotional moments of communication. In addition, interpretation always takes into account the context of meaning in which an action stands. Understanding the context requires recognising the motives for an action. Only in this way does interpretation lead to the construction of meaning. The dimensions of understanding, comprehension and grasping the context can be affected by off-site communication.

As we have seen, the aim of *questioning* is to gather information and clarify facts. The interviewer or the courts often have to determine what they consider true or false, as interviewees give different and at times conflicting information. This may be due to them having perceived the situation subjectively differently, or they might be intentionally lying for a number of reasons. To evaluate the veracity of a statement, the *questioner* assesses all the information they have received, not only the verbal, but also the non-verbal and the extra-verbal elements. Interpreting is based on domain knowledge, technical language and cultural competence, with information being processed both at the cognitive and the emotional levels. Interpreters work in different domains, and often in contexts that include more than one technical field, and their work is always also cooperation with the professionals of those fields.

Interprofessional cooperation takes place in both the social and the technical contexts. Many expert actions also involve several domains; in this book, we have considered in particular legal (including criminological and psychological) and translatorial aspects. Knowledge of the other profession, coordinated action and, ideally, connectivity of the professions involved already established in training (cf. Kadrić, Rennert and Mikić, 2021) supports the emergence of transdisciplines. Although the rapid advancement especially of automation and the increased use of technology have accelerated communication considerably and allow it to ignore location constraints and borders, they also complicate interpersonal communication through the emergence of special forms of communication, turning communication itself into a hybrid phenomenon.

Questioning and interpreting as special forms of communication result (together) in a hybrid phenomenon. This form of communication is already in itself a hybrid due to the fact that it does not take place directly, but through third parties. There are a number of hybrid forms of communication; the following are particularly relevant for legal and official proceedings: hybridity of media, hybridity of text and discourse modalities, and hybridity of interpreting modes.

7.2 Hybridity of media and the increasing use of technology in communication

Hybridity in technology-assisted communication arises from the integration of information and communication technologies (ICT) into the communication process. ICT are used both for interviews themselves and for remote interpreting, as well as for preparation and debriefing.

Remote communication, whether by audio or by video link, is a hybrid form. The participants are not all physically in the same place, which poses a number of challenges that are not present in traditional onsite communication.

With the use of information and communication technologies, an interview and/or its interpretation can take place via video or audio link from another room, another building or even a different country. Due to the use of technology, the interviewees are no longer bound by spatial constraints. The requirements for the participants also differ depending on the type of technology used.

Two main reasons for using ICT in official procedures are: (1) to enable communication at a distance (e.g. for health reasons); and (2) to increase efficiency and productivity (e.g. by saving time and resources).

There is a wide range of uses for technology-supported communication at courts and authorities. In court proceedings, video conferencing enables jurors or witnesses to participate in proceedings without having to travel. It is even possible to pronounce a judgement via video conferencing. This not only facilitates access to justice, but also the application of the law. Especially in rural areas, technology can help improve access to justice or even make it possible in the first place. This helps avoid conflicts of interest particularly in small (linguistic) communities in rural areas by making it easier to organise jurisdiction elsewhere (particularly relevant in the case of interpreting). The use of unbiased experts from outside the community via audio or video link allows access to the legal system while respecting the rights of all parties involved. Courts or authorities are also increasingly resorting to video hearings for witnesses from outside the country and waive the right to summon the witnesses to appear before the recording court in person. In such cases, they need to decide whether the interpreter is present at the court where the witness is being heard or at the recognising court.

Technologies enable and shape communication. Dialogue interpreting requires its own *questioning* and interpreting strategies tailored to the technology. For example, using eye contact to signal turn taking is not possible. In communication transmitted via audio or video link, it is necessary to consider which non-verbal and extra-verbal communication elements the other participants can perceive and which not. Visual communication elements, naturally, are not visible in audio-mediated communication and therefore cannot be used. Even in video-mediated communication, the section that the camera transmits must be considered, as non-verbal and extra-verbal communication outside the camera image is not visible to the other person and therefore cannot be perceived. Cross-talk can lead to a loss of information, as not everyone can be heard. We see that although technology enables communication and interpreting over distances, it also influences them significantly. It might, for example, be necessary to verbalise or explicitate content that is not visible but is essential for communication, so that the other person receives it. Thus, communication with technology differs fundamentally from communication without technology. It therefore stands to reason that video-based interpreting, too, is different from onsite interpreting.

The use of technology enables the acceleration of work processes and more efficient use of resources. However, it is necessary to consider in which situations the use of technology adds value and in which it hinders the communication process. In addition to ensuring that it does not run counter to the purpose of communication, it is also necessary to check whether those involved in the communication are familiar with the technology or if it might present an additional obstacle for them.

Growing digitalisation means that digital skills are becoming increasingly taken for granted. It is to be expected that along with the increased use of technology, the expectation of digital competences will rise for experts in various fields, including legal experts and interpreters. The technical requirements of the video-based communicative situation limit the possibilities of perception compared to situations in which interpretation takes place on site. Information can only be perceived through two information channels: auditory and visual. This circumstance requires other communication strategies adapted to the technology. With regard to strategies, it is important to consider not only quality but also the well-being of those involved in the communication.

The use of technology can be an additional burden and cause increased stress. Studies have shown that interpreters working remotely experience higher physical and psychological strain than when interpreting on site. Creating a good remote working environment and preparing terminology and topics contribute significantly to relieving the stress. Talking with colleagues and other experts can have a positive effect on well-being.

Technology-assisted communication (including interpreting) via audio and video therefore differs from onsite communication in four essential points:

Interpreting strategies: technology-assisted communication requires communication strategies adapted to the technology. It involves a series of sequential and parallel activities and is always tied to the particular communication medium used.

Digital competences: Technology-supported communication requires digital competences in order to be able to use the technology effectively.

Perception: In remote communication, perception is determined by the technology used. Thus, in telephone interpreting, perception is exclusively possible through the auditory channel, while via video, only a small section of the interpreting situation is visible. There may be a lack of information that needs to be bridged, including missing explicit and implicit information.

Cognitive load: Technology-enhanced communication can place a higher strain on the participants, as they have to deal with technical challenges and provide a high-quality service at the same time.

The use of technology opens up the possibility for hybrid forms of communication that have different constellations. For example, participants may be present in one location while the interpreter is connected remotely, or the participants may be in two or more different locations. The visual and auditory cues that can be perceived vary depending on the constellation, necessitating an adaptation of communication strategies.

In this sense, hybridity of communication is a dynamic concept that involves the merging of onsite and offsite communication to enable effective communication across distances.

7.3 Hybridity of modalities: written/oral

In most proceedings, texts are transformed from the oral to the written form and vice versa. The oral proceedings are usually documented by means of a written transcript. A large part of the evidence might already be available in writing. Thus, spoken language is written down and written texts are reproduced orally. This influences not only the use of language, but also the interpreting process, and highlights another important (hybrid) form of interpreting that is important in practice: *sight interpreting* (see for more Chapter 3).

In court and official settings, interviews are documented in written form to be used in the further course of the proceedings. This is a transfer of orally presented content into a written form. The person conducting the interview is responsible for the transcript, either themselves or assisted by a clerk. In some cases, interpreters may adapt their interpretation for the transcript in such a way that the oral text is given characteristics of written text, so the statement is recorded in the transcript in a more formal language than it was uttered. In certain situations, the law provides for the finished transcript to be back-translated for the party giving the statement. Sight interpreting is also used in other situations, e.g. to ensure someone understands documents used in the proceedings. Sight interpreting is a special form of simultaneous interpreting. Content that is present in a permanent written form is reproduced orally under time constraints. In this hybrid form of interpreting, the source information is recorded visually, processed cognitively and reproduced in the target language. In the course of this process, the perspective changes, along with function of the text: The interpreted version of the document is an informative text with a reporting function, intended to make what has just been presented by the representative of the authority or the court comprehensible to the user of a language other than the *language of service*. The interpreter addresses this user only. Thus, the impersonal information in the interpretation is personalised, as we saw in the *customised interpreting* example in Chapter 3.

Recent technological applications have given rise to the hybrid mode of Sight-Consec. Here, an oral source text is transcribed into a written text using automatic speech recognition. The transcribed source text is then consecutively sight interpreted into the target language, back into spoken form. This technology-assisted form does not rely on pre-existing written documents; this text is created directly in the interpreting situation to support the interpreter and can be combined with the interpreter's handwritten notes As with other technology-assisted forms of communication where recordings are made, permission for the technology-assisted recording of the source speech contributions must be obtained from all participants. When using prepared texts, it is important to note that speakers frequently diverge from these scripts, which can impose an extra cognitive burden on interpreters, similar to the load that computer-assisted interpretation (CAI) tools may introduce.

The multi-faceted nature of interpreters' tasks in court or official proceedings means that their work encompasses various forms of translatorial activity.

Another special hybrid form of translation is found in the surveillance of legal wiretapping. Communication surveillance in pre-trial proceedings and investigations is carried out with the help of interpreters whenever the investigators do not understand the language of the intercepted communication.

In communication surveillance, intercepted audio information is processed and, if necessary, documented in writing for further use in the proceedings. The interlingual transfer of an oral conversation into a written document is complex and is influenced by several factors. Since audio information can contain linguistic as well as non-linguistic and extra-linguistic cues, there is not only an interlingual transfer, from one language to another, but also an intermodal transfer, from oral to written language.

7.4 Hybridity of modes: simultaneous/consecutive interpreting

The use of technology also enables other forms of hybrid interpretation. For example, both simultaneous and consecutive interpreting can be combined. In the hybrid interpreting mode SimConsec, a speech is reproduced consecutively as simultaneous interpreting. For this purpose, the speech is recorded with an audio recording device that also allows the interpreter to take notes and stores the notes digitally, usually a so-called smart pen or a tablet. When one is using the smart pen, which is an audio recording device with a ballpoint pen tip, notes are taken in analogue mode on a paper notepad specifically designed for this purpose. If digital note-taking is preferred, a stylus can be used on a tablet in a note-taking app with a recording function. In both cases, the notes are linked to the audio recording of the original speech, so that it is possible to play the part of the audio recording associated with a specific point in the notes at any time.

Due to data protection regulations, the unrestricted use of recording devices is not possible. Recordings are only permitted with the consent of all participants. In (data) sensitive settings, e.g. with medical or criminal content, the use of electronic devices may be denied. Even the use of analogue notepads may be restricted in some settings to the extent that the notes must be handed over after completion of the interpreting assignment or destroyed on site. The hybrid interpreting mode SimConsec is especially useful for didactic purposes, as the ability to play back the recording and the digital notes enables a step-by-step analysis of the cognitive processes during note-taking. Playing back the notes together with the recording can also be used to analyse notes or to demonstrate the time lag between speech and note-taking.

Study activities

- *Technology-assisted interpreting*
  - List settings where audio or video-mediated interpreting is used.
  - Interactive exercise: Set up a video link between two separate rooms. Compare the interpreting conditions under different scenarios. Contrast the scenario where the interpreter is present at the same location as the *questioner* with the scenario where the interpreter is connected remotely.
    - What challenges arise for the participants when interpreting is done remotely compared to the scenario where the interpreter is present onsite with one of the parties involved in the conversation?
    - How is the turn-taking of speakers coordinated?
    - Describe the perception of visual information from a remote location and at the shared location with one of the parties involved in the conversation.
  - Conduct a gap analysis for the use of technology in interpreting:
    - Current state: Describe the present technologies and methods being used in the field of interpreting.
    - Desired state: Outline the ideal scenarios or objectives that should be achieved with the implementation of new or improved technologies.
    - Gaps analysis: Identify the discrepancies or 'gaps' between the current and desired states.
    - Measures to close the gaps (evaluation and creation): Propose or recommend strategies, processes or technologies that could be implemented to close the identified gaps.

This structured task description can serve as a guideline for conducting a comprehensive gap analysis in the context of the use of technology in interpreting.

Sources and further reading

Capus, N. and Havelka, I. (2021) 'Interpreting Intercepted Communication: A Sui Generis Translational Activity' *International Journal for the Semiotiocs in Law* https://doi.org/10.1007/s11196-021-09876-0.

Goldsmith, J. (2018) 'Tablet Interpreting: Consecutive Interpreting 2.0' *Translation and Interpreting Studies*, 13(3), pp. 342–65 https://doi.org/10.1075/tis.00020.gol

Havelka, I., Iacono, K., Pöllabauer, S. and Stachl (2022) 'Distance interpreting in asylum proceedings' in *UNHCR: Handbook for Interpreters in Asylum Procedures*. 2nd and revised edition, pp. 215–41. Frank & Timme.

Havnen, R. (2019) 'Multimodal and Interactional Aspects of Sight Translation: A Critical Review' *FITISPos-IJ*, 6(1), pp. 91–106 https://doi.org/10.37536/FITISPos-IJ.2019.6.1.206

Kadrić, M. (2021) 'Legal Interpreting and Social Discourse', In: Ji, M. and Laviosa, S. (eds.) *The Oxford Handbook of Translation and Social Practices*. Oxford University Press, pp. 500–20.

Kadrić, M., Rennert, S. and Mikić, D. (2021) 'Connected education and co-construction of knowledge in a joint course for law and interpreting students' *Linguistica Antverpiensia*, New Series: Themes in Translation Studies, 20 https://doi.org/10.52034/lanstts.v20i.610.

Stempkowski, M. and Grafl, C. (2021) 'Dolmetschen und Lügenerkennung' in K. Kaindl, S. Pöllabauer and D. Mikić (eds.), *Dolmetschen als Dienst am Menschen*. Texte für Mira Kadrić, pp. 161–73. Narr Francke Attempto.

techforword. (n.d.). SightConsec: Use automatic speech recognition to improve your consecutive interpreting. [online] https://www.techforword.com/blog/sightconsec-use-automatic-speech-recognition-to-improve-your-consecutive-interpreting (accessed 27 September 2023).

Conclusion

Questioning and interpreting as two sides of the same communication coin

As we have seen, questioning is one of the most important methods that courts and authorities have when it comes to gathering information and collecting evidence. Accordingly, questioning techniques are very important. The fields of criminology and jurisprudence both use questioning and draw conclusions based on it, although their perspectives and emphases differ.

The interpreter's goal is always to ensure the best possible communication. To do so, the interpreter has to understand the communication strategies being used. Therefore, it is not sufficient for an interpreter in a legal setting to have a basic understanding of legal terminology and law; he also has to understand the questioning strategies and types of discourse used in legal proceedings, as well as the underlying criminological and psychological factors.

Language is an inseparable part of communication. Language competence as part of communicative competence is of particular importance. Language competence is a term that can be used to explain and define what we mean when we talk about a profound mastery of a language. Profound mastery includes both the active mastery of the language and the explicit understanding of that language and of professional, social and cultural aspects of how that language is used. This involves the conscious, pragmatic, social and cultural ability to apply language systematically to different situations and subject areas. Working with language(s) at courts and authorities takes place against the background of patterns of thought and perception as information processing, with the additional need to take typical subject- and role-specific conventions of texts and their connections into account.

Linguistic competence is also the basis of interpreting competence. The prerequisite for translatorial work in a languages pair is mastery of these languages a sound knowledge not only of vocabulary, stylistic devices and grammar, but also of technical, everyday, dialect and regional language usage. This kind of language mastery also implies conscious language use and awareness of the culture-specific perceptions in different languages. This requires first the assignment of the conceptual-semantic considerations to the respective cultural framework, which enables us to abstract from our own cultural influences so that we can examine the social meaning of the texts within a (professional) culture.

DOI: 10.4324/9781003301585-9

The structures in judicial and official proceedings and the interaction between the actors involved contribute significantly to the success of the communication. On the example of questioning, we have shown that all actors actively involved in triadic communication (initiating speech act, response, reproduction of initiating speech act and response) are taking two actions simultaneously: They act and react on the topic at hand and they steer the conversation implicitly and explicitly.

All participants make pre-planned and situational strategic decisions and share responsibility for the success (and often the outcome) of the communication. In doing so, they use various instruments of a linguistic, non-linguistic and extralinguistic nature. This allows them to actively participate in the interaction and co-construct meaning.

The interaction format and the official interaction context determine the type of interaction, the framework within which the participants can operate and the means available to the participants in a given situation. The interaction format, the official context and the individual interests of the parties are a guideline for how information is handled and in what way content is prepared and communicated. Especially in interview situations, there is a strong interdependence between perception, memory and linguistic reproduction of information.

Advancing digitalisation, mobility, growing tourism, trade, migration and refugee movements also mean more communication, be it on site or remote. In judicial or administrative proceedings, a high degree of accuracy is expected from all parties involved. The understanding of fundamental rights, of the right to a fair trial and the increasing demand for quality assurance and professionalisation of communication increase the overall quality of the proceedings. The courts and authorities as well as the public rely on experts in this regard. Therefore, both courts and authorities and people seeking justice have a right to expect that the persons working for the authorities or offering their services have the necessary qualifications and integrity to do so. The rights of the individual, regardless of their nationality or language skills, must not suffer from a lack of communication or misunderstanding. Conversely, unambiguous communication supports the courts and authorities and enables proceedings to run smoothly – with or without technology.

Glossary

adversarial system Mainly used in common law countries. The parties to the trial mainly determine its content. The court as an impartial institution ensures compliance with procedure. Considering evidence follows complex rules.

case law, also common law Legal system used in Anglo-American countries. The main source of law are previous court decisions (precedents).

civil law Legal system used in most of continental Europe, South America and parts of Asia and Africa. Codified legal norms represent the highest legal authority, prescribing rules in an abstract manner.

customised interpreting Type of interpreting where the optimisation of comprehensibility of a spoken or signed text or discourse is the primary concern, considering the meaning of the message as a whole ('free interpreting').

distance interpreting Interpreting situation in which the interpreter and at least one end-user of interpreting services are in different locations and are connected by information and communication technology.

duplication Duplication refers to the repetition of information in a different form, specifically when a technical term is initially presented using technical language and is subsequently reiterated in everyday language.

end-user of legal interpreting services Any person for whom interpreting services related to law or legal matters are intended.

inquisitorial system Mainly used in civil law countries. The court is responsible for conducting legal proceedings during the trial. Only a few rules apply regarding the assessment of evidence.

language of service Language of procedure, usually an official language or a language required to facilitate communication agreed upon in advance or required for the individual communicative setting.

legal interpreting Interpreting in communicative contexts related to law and legal matters, regardless of whether the client is a public institution or a private individual or entity.

lingua franca Language of communication in a multilingual area in which at least two people speaking different languages can communicate in a common language without the involvement or help of third parties.

multipartiality Interpreters align themselves equally with all parties in a discussion, serving the interests of each. By upholding professional equidistance and presenting all viewpoints evenly, interpreters build confidence and establish trust. Multipartiality prioritises the user and their communication requirements. (Term used instead of impartiality.)

preserved interpreting Type of interpreting that where a spoken or signed text or discourse is rendered as unchanged in form and content as possible ('literal interpreting').

questioning Hearings, interviews or interrogations in a legal context that serve to clarify a matter.

questionee A person who is questioned in a context related to law or a legal matter to clarify a fact.

questioner A person who conducts hearings, interviews or interrogations and is officially authorised to do so.

sight interpreting Also known as 'prima vista' or 'sight translation', this refers to the immediate and on-the-spot interpretation of a written text from one language to another. This type of interpreting involves reading a text in one language and simultaneously orally rendering the meaning in another language, without prior exposure to the content.

tandem Tandem exercises are a pair-based collaborative learning strategy where two learners with complementary skills or knowledge work together to teach and learn from each other.

text (source, target, written, oral, signed) A written, spoken or signed element of language that conveys a record of content. It may also refer more broadly to any written, spoken or symbolic representation of language that conveys meaning.

translatorial rapport Supporting the end-users in establishing and maintaining communication (on a factual and relational level) despite the language barrier. Establishing and maintaining communication between the interpreter and the end-users.

triadic communication Communication that, at its core, takes place between two people in which a third person is involved for certain reasons (e.g. because of the language barrier).

Index

For Product Safety Concerns and Information please contact our EU representative GPSR@taylorandfrancis.com
Taylor & Francis Verlag GmbH, Kaufingerstraße 24, 80331 München, Germany

www.ingramcontent.com/pod-product-compliance
Ingram Content Group UK Ltd.
Pitfield, Milton Keynes, MK11 3LW, UK
UKHW020000200926
475702UK00015B/2389
9781032294414